Living in the Conversation

*Keys to Creative Preaching
and Worship in
Small Membership Churches*

James L. Killen Jr.

CSS Publishing Company, Inc.
Lima, Ohio

LIVING IN THE CONVERSATION

FIRST EDITION
Copyright © 2014
by CSS Publishing Co., Inc.

Published by CSS Publishing Company, Inc., Lima, Ohio 45807. All rights reserved. No part of this publication may be reproduced in any manner whatsoever without the prior permission of the publisher, except in the case of brief quotations embodied in critical articles and reviews. Inquiries should be addressed to: CSS Publishing Company, Inc., Permissions Department, 5450 N. Dixie Highway, Lima, Ohio 45807.

Library of Congress Cataloging-in-Publication Data

Killen, James L.
   Living in the conversation : keys to creative preaching and worship in small membership churches / James Killen, Jr. -- FIRST EDITION.
     pages cm
   ISBN 0-7880-2773-5 (alk. paper)
 1. Small churches. 2. Public worship. 3. Preaching. I. Title.

   BV637.8.K54   2014
   264--dc23

                                                    2013038206

For more information about CSS Publishing Company resources, visit our website at www.csspub.com, email us at csr@csspub.com, or call (800) 241-4056.

e-book:
ISBN-13: 978-0-7880-2774-1
ISBN-10: 0-7880-2774-3

ISBN-13: 978-0-7880-2773-4
ISBN-10: 0-7880-2773-5   PRINTED IN USA

Table of Contents

Introduction	5
The Big Question	11
Creative Faithfulness	15
Living in the Conversation	19
Designing an Order of Worship	27
Developing an Appreciation for the Dynamics of Worship	31
Beginning to Plan Services of Worship	35
Preparing to Preach	47
Planning Sermons	51
Discovering the Message	59
Developing a Structure for Your Sermon	67
Gathering Material for Building the Sermon	71
Presenting the Sermon	83
How to Preach on Controversial Issues and Survive	89
Preparing a Service of Worship	91
Preparing Prayers	101
Preaching and Worship in the Real World	107

Introduction

"How was church today?" Bill Anderson was talking to his dad on a Sunday afternoon while their wives put Sunday dinner on the table. Bill had grown up going to the open country church in Johnson's Prairie, but a few years ago he and his family moved to the small town of Waycross fifteen miles away and started going to the church in town. He was still interested in his home church, so as he sat in his parent's living room he asked, "How was church today?"

His dad answered, "Oh, it was about like it's been a-bein'. The preacher had someone play a record of an orchestra playin' praise choruses and then fussed at us because we didn't sing loud enough. Then when he preached he paced back and forth, wavin' his arms and shoutin' like a TV evangelist. I'm afraid we are a big disappointment to him."

Bill asked, "Doesn't he let Aunt Sally play the hymns on the piano any more?"

"No, she just doesn't do to suit him. Her feelings are really hurt, but she doesn't say anythin' about it."

"What do you think he has on his mind?"

"I don't know. I think he thinks he has to win converts and turn our little church into a great big church, but I don't see that happenin'. Some people like what he is doin' and they brag on him. That just makes him more determined. To tell you the truth, I don't get much out of his sermons. He is a good young guy and he means well, but I keep wantin' to tell him, 'Son there ain't but thirty of us here and we are all already Christians. Don't you have somethin' to say to us?' "

Bill shook his head and said, "I'm sorry to hear that. I'll always love the Johnson's Prairie Church."

Bill's dad asked, "How was church in Waycross?"

Bill answered, "Different from that. It's hard to believe that the two churches are of the same denomination. Our preacher does everything by the book, wears a robe, reads four scripture lessons every Sunday, has us reading prayers and stuff."

Bill's dad nodded, "How about the sermon?"

"Oh, he always has somethin' good to say. You can tell he has studied and thought it through. He has it all written out up there. He reads it to us, never looks up. He always does what he's supposed to do, but to tell you the truth, I liked church more when the other pastor was there. She was a little looser, a little warmer."

The subject of the conversation was preaching and worship. Lots of conversations take place on that subject. Thousands of people go to church every Sunday in churches of every size and description. They go because they think it is important and because they expect something significant to happen there. They may not have a very clear idea of what they expect to happen, but they keep hoping it will. And they talk about it. We are going to talk about it too.

This is a book about preaching and worship. It is especially about preaching and worship in small membership churches with an average attendance of less than 100 — and that is most of them. This book is especially for pastors and for others who have responsibility for planning and leading services of worship and for preaching. It is introductory. It is especially for beginners. But some who are old hands at preaching and worship might pick up a few insights along the way.

Your author is a person with 45 years of experience in preaching and in planning and leading services of worship. I spent a number of years serving small membership churches, then I served three middle-sized churches, and finally two fairly large churches. I am grateful for all of those experiences, because I believe that each of them gave me an opportunity to invest my life in the most important thing that is going on in the world. Each of them also taught me valuable lessons. I have seen a number of liturgical "styles" come and go, and I learned from each of them. Along the way, I earned a Doctor of Ministry degree in preaching and worship from an excellent seminary and I have written sermons and sermon resources for publication.

In "retirement" I am again being called on to fill the pulpits of small membership churches while their pastors are away. Sometimes there are half a dozen people there and sometimes half a hundred or more. I am glad to accept those invitations because I believe that each of those occasions has the possibility of being the time when something really significant may happen. Each of the people there is a unique individual. Each is playing out a unique drama in his or her life. Each is participating in some ways, sometimes in very significant ways, in the greater drama of human life and history. Each has gone to the trouble to come to church, expecting that something significant may happen there. Many of them have made costly commitments to keeping their churches alive and serving. Each person and each gathering is unique. They have their unique ways of doing worship. But I am convinced that each of those gatherings of people has the potential for being an effective agent of God's loving work in the world.

I am also convinced that, even in this world where bigness is thought to represent success, the small membership churches have a very special role to play in the total mission of God's people in the world. Small membership churches have to work with some limitations, but they also get to work with some unique possibilities. In the small membership church, the weekly service of preaching and worship is the most important thing that happens. If something really significant is going to happen in these congregations or in the lives of their members, it is most likely to happen in the Sunday worship service. And if the church has any potential for growth of any kind, that potential is most likely to be realized through what happens in the worship service.

I believe that the preaching and worship by the church is one of the most important things going on in the world. It can be one of God's most effective tools in saving people — and humankind — from the messes we keep making of life to the fullness of life that God wants for us all. It deserves the very best efforts of all who are involved in it in any way. I have never stopped being excited about it.

There are two problems that an author must confront when writing a book on preaching and worship. One is that many people will start by asking where the author stands with regard to the conflict currently going on in the church that has been called "the worship wars." They are asking if the author is an advocate of contemporary or traditional worship, of organs and robes or guitars and golf shirts. Please don't ask that. We will soon get around to suggesting a way of planning worship that is very different from just choosing a style and following it. Be ready to take a really fresh approach to planning preaching and worship.

The other problem with writing a book on preaching and worship is that most of the people who read it will think that they already know all — or almost all — that they need to know about it. You have participated in worship and heard preaching. You have seen it done and had it done to you. You think that you can do what you have seen done. In fact, you may have a secret (or not so secret) belief that you can do it better than some of the people you have seen doing it. When you have had an opportunity to try it, your friends and relatives came around and told you that it was wonderful and you chose to believe them. Well, you may indeed know all you need to know about preaching and worship, but do me a favor — for the sake of the usefulness of this book, pretend you don't.

This book is going to be a very basic introduction. I will begin by asking some questions that lots of people involved in preaching and worship have forgotten to ask, about what preaching and worship is all about and what we should expect to happen in it. When there is some clarity about what we are supposed to be doing, I will talk about the practicalities of how to do it. I will try to put a lot of things into perspective in a short time. Even if you are a seasoned professional, if you choose to invest your energy in reading this book, start by pretending that you are a beginner. You may make some discoveries along the way.

One thing will be a little unique about this book, beside its very introductory character. In most cases, when you read about preaching and worship you have to read about them in two separate books. That is simply because the people who write those books tend to be specialists in one field or the other. But *most* preaching takes place within the worship service of a congregation and is done by the pastor who serves that congregation. Most people experience preaching and worship as one unit and as an expression of the total life of the church. We will see that there are some real advantages in preparing a service of preaching and worship as a unit and in doing it in, with, and for the congregation.

In this book, I am going to share lots of things I have learned by reading books about preaching and worship, and also lots of things I have learned by doing it. Sometimes I have learned by doing things incorrectly several times before I got them right. That seems to be my style in learning. I will also be sharing some insights that I have gained by teaching in the schools that my denomination provides for pastors who are not going to seminary.

In addition to the sharing of insights and instructions, I have included some worksheets at the end of the chapters that will invite you to use the things about which you have been reading in preparing a sermon and a service of worship. I hope that you will find them useful.

I feel that I have a lot to share with you. Just so you can be sure to get the point, I will occasionally include little summary statements in bold print which I am calling "keys to creative preaching and worship." You will recognize them because they will look like this:

> **Stay excited**
> **about the possibility**
> **that is always present**
> **when people gather**
> **to worship the living God.**

The Big Question

Let's start by asking the big question. What is supposed to happen in preaching and worship? What is it supposed to accomplish? What should the participants come expecting? It will be important to know this information so that we can prepare to do appropriate things as we plan and participate in preaching and worship. Then we can know how to evaluate its effectiveness.

It is surprising how many people participate in services of preaching and worship, and even in the actual preaching and leadership of worship, without asking and answering that question. They simply go through the motions they have seen others go through, or they have been taught to go through without asking why. Then they sometimes put their own personal "spin" on the processes for their own personal reasons. Going through expected motions without asking why is not the best way to give leadership in preaching and worship.

What is supposed to happen in preaching and worship? Are these activities supposed to instruct, inspire, entertain, make converts, promote some cause or program, and build up the institutional church? Soon after I had come to a new parish, one of the ladies of the church (who eventually became my close friend) complained to me about the Christmas Eve service that had been held the previous year. I asked what had been done. She told me. It sounded all right to me, so I asked, "Just what is it that you expect of a Christmas Eve service?" Without a moment's hesitation, she answered, "Goosebumps! I expect a Christmas Eve service to give me goosebumps." A service of preaching and worship can do a lot of things. It may even give you goosebumps, but none of the things we have mentioned can be an adequate statement of the purpose of preaching and worship. The purpose has to be something much bigger.

In preaching and worship, something important is supposed to happen between people and God.

We live every day of our lives in some kind of a relationship with God. We might even argue that all of our daily interactions with life *are* interactions with God — whether or not we know it — whether or not we even believe in God. Those interactions — what we believe about that with which we are interacting, and how we choose to respond — shape our lives. This actually is going on all the time, whether or not we are conscious of it. The Christian faith teaches us that there actually is someone out there in and behind all of the little things with which we interact daily, someone who is interacting with us through them, and that someone is God.

The Christian faith teaches us certain things to believe about the God who meets us and interacts with us through all of the experiences and relationships of life. It teaches us that God is real, God is alive and active and intentional, and above all God is loving.

It also teaches us that there are certain ways in which we should respond to God and to life. We should respond in openness, trust, commitment, and love.

The Christian faith teaches us that if we let those beliefs and responses shape our lives, we will be able to move into a right relationship with God and with life. We will be able to find our ways into life at its best that the Bible calls by such names as "fullness of life" or "the new life of the kingdom of God" or "eternal life."

Well, if all of that happens in our everyday interactions with life, why do we need services of preaching and worship? Because some folks haven't heard what the Christian faith has to tell us about God and about how we should respond to God. And some who have heard haven't yet fully moved into relationship with God that can lead to fullness of life. Many who have heard what the Christian faith teaches and have believed it have chosen to let it shape their lives, yet are having a hard time doing so because they live in a world that hasn't heard about God and isn't living in faith and in love. It is important to come away occasionally to remember God and all that the Christian faith has taught us about

God. We need to renew our relationship with God and to grow in it so that we can go back out into the real world and live lives shaped by a trusting and loving relationship with God. That is what is supposed to happen in preaching and worship.

Does that shed some new light on the subject?

> **It is important
> to remember that God
> is a participant
> in our preaching and worship.**

We must remember that this God, about whom we will be talking and to whom we will be witnessing, and whose relationship with us we will be dramatizing, is real, alive, present, and active. This means that we who preach and lead worship are never really in control of the situation. God is alive and beyond our control. As a matter of fact, so are the people to whom we will be speaking and whom we will lead in worship. The best we can do is try to facilitate an interaction between people and God. In that sentence, the expression "the best we can do" is not meant to belittle the activity to which it is applied. Facilitating an interaction between people and God really is the very best thing that we can do. **Write that down and underline it.** That is the job of the preacher and of those who lead worship. We facilitate a potentially life-shaping interaction between people and God.

Then what should we expect to come of it? We can't really control that either. It is like introducing two people to one another and then allowing the relationship to develop as they choose to let it. It will go where God and the people involved need for it to go or choose to let it go. We may ask whether or not the service instructed, inspired, entertained, made converts, promoted causes, or built up the body of the church. We may even ask whether it gave anyone goosebumps. We may use some of those things or hope that some of those things will come from the service. But to intentionally organize the service of worship to accomplish such things, or to evaluate the service in terms of whether or not they were accomplished, would be wrong. The interactions between people and God have a life of their own. They go where they need to go. Ultimately we will want to ask: Are the people who participate in worship living free, trusting, and loving lives? Are they building more just and loving communities? Are they building a more just and loving world? If we have to evaluate the results, these are the criteria that the Bible suggests. (See 1 Corinthians 13.)

> **Remember what it is supposed to be all about.**
> **Preaching and worship are supposed to help something happen between people and God that will shape their lives and maybe guide human history.**

Creative Faithfulness

I would like to suggest a particular way of approaching the task of preparing for preaching and worship. I call it "creative faithfulness."

During the days of Christian existentialism, there was a theologian by the name of Nicolas Berdyaev[1] who advocated an ethic of creativity. Contrary to what you might think, he used the word "creative" not to represent something that is always new or avantgarde, but rather to represent what is really appropriate in any real-life situation. He was saying that instead of simply applying any cut-and-dried set of rules, a person ought to try to thoroughly understand the dynamics of every aspect of any real-life situation and then do what was really called for from a Christian in that situation. It might be something old and traditional. It might be something brand-new and never heard of before. The norm of that Christian action is love.

It seems to me that we can use the same kind of creativity in planning preaching and worship. Instead of doing what has always been done, getting out the Anglican *Book of Common Prayer* or referring to the latest publications on contemporary worship, we should try hard to understand the dynamic dimensions of the worship situation and all of the aspects of the Christian faith that we hope to communicate. Then do what seems most appropriate and most effective in that situation. Whereas the norm of Christian ethics should be love, the norm of Christian worship should be faithfulness. We must be faithful to the Christian witness to God that we find in the Bible and in the traditions and experiences of the church. We must also be faithful to the people who come to church hoping to be led into a relationship with God. None of the traditions of worship should rule us. But all of the traditions of Christian worship should be available to us. We should actually strive to know and to do what is most appropriate in every worship situation. That is what I mean by creative faithfulness. It is much more work than simply following one tradition, but it can make preaching and worship much more relevant and exciting. Let's try it.

> **Real creativity is doing
> what is appropriate.
> Let creative faithfulness
> be your method and your style
> in planning preaching and worship.**

Let me give you an example of what I mean. I frequently find myself worshiping in four different settings. The church service I usually attend each Sunday is held in a magnificent sanctuary where people sing traditional hymns to the music of a grand organ as the choir processes with great dignity down the center aisle. When it is time to pray, people kneel on kneelers that are built into the pews and sometimes read prayers from the printed bulletin. You get the picture, don't you?

That same church also holds services in that same room to meet the felt needs of another group of people in the same congregation, or maybe a different set of felt needs in the lives of the people who usually attend the other services. The service is less formal. People sing a different style of song while reading the words projected on a screen. The pastor leaves the pulpit and speaks as he walks around the chancel area. You get that picture too, don't you?

I also occasionally worship with a group of people who are participants in the "Walk to Emmaus." That is similar to the Cursillo retreats that some other churches have. They are a retreat setting intended to provide spiritual renewal for people who are already active in churches. They practice a kind of worship that combines informative talks with the rituals of the sacrament of the Lord's Supper plus some gospel songs and praise choruses sung to the music of guitars.

The fourth worship setting I find myself in is that of a prison ministry. There the purpose is evangelistic. Worship services are designed to lead people who are not Christians into the Christian faith and to reinforce their faith so they can live it under difficult circumstances. There is no use of the sacraments. Evangelistic talks are combined with singing that sometimes leads men starved for human intimacy to put their arms around one another to form a circle as they sing, and that may let men who have no opportunity for emotional release to get caught up in dancing and laughing.

Which of those styles of worship is right? I believe they all are. They are all appropriate and effective in the settings for which they are designed and for the people they are designed to serve. All of them embody authentic expressions of the Christian faith. It might be stimulating to occasionally borrow something from one of those worship settings and use it in one of the others. But to take one of those styles of worship and impose it upon one of the other settings could be completely counterproductive. It would not meet needs and it would not be appropriate. Creativity in planning preaching and worship should be a matter of carefully understanding the dynamics of each worship setting and then choosing, or creating, acts of worship that are appropriate.

---

1. Nicolas Berdyaev, *The Destiny of Man.*

Living in the Conversation

It should be clear that preaching and leading worship is not just something you can stand up and do once, twice, or three times a week. To do them well requires many hours of preparation. To do them as they should be done requires that they become a way of life for those who do them. Preaching and worship have to do with interaction with the living God. They are particular, intentional interactions intended to sensitize us to the greater interaction that is going on all the time in our lives and to help us live out that interaction in ways that will lead us into fullness of life. Our preparation to preach or to lead worship needs to be informed and guided by a kind of ongoing conversation between the Christian faith's witness to God and our experience of life.

> **The best way
> to begin your preparation
> is to live every day
> in the conversation
> between life and the Christian witness.**

Learn to experience life in depth. Live your own life in depth. Dare to be aware of all that is happening in your own life and to feel it. Ponder its meaning. Take in every bit of the beauty and the grandeur of life. It is a gift from God. Let it enable you. Dare to embrace any pain or tragedy and the demands that may be parts of your life. They too are parts of the gift. They will help you to grow. Incorporate these things into your devotional life. Develop the habit of talking them all over with God. Be honest with God about what is going on in your life, then be quiet and listen to see what God may have to say in response. It would be a mistake to think that everyone else is having experiences just like yours. But you can know that every other person is living out some life drama, just as you are. Experiencing your own life in depth will prepare you to be sensitive and responsive to the things that are going on in the lives of others.

Your work as a pastor or as a caring church member should enable you to get a feeling for the drama that is going on in the lives of people who are parts of your congregation and community. These are the people whom you will serve with your preaching and leadership of worship. They are the ones whose daily interactions with life need to be shaped into interactions with the God who loves them. Listen to the things they tell you about what is going on in their lives and how they are feeling about it and what they may be thinking it means. They *will* tell you. They may not tell you directly in so many words, but in some ways by attitudes, actions, what they don't say, and many other ways. They will tell you because they want you to know. Listen to them. Listen as you visit in the hospital rooms. Listen as you drink coffee with the good old boys. Listen when things go sour in a business meeting. Listen, listen, listen. Listen and build a composite understanding of the drama that is going on in the lives of the individuals around you and in the life of the congregation and the community you serve.

It is also important for you to live in conversation with the things that are going on in the wider world. Whether or not they know it, the people you serve are participants in the greater drama of human life and history. Things that happen in the wider world will impact their lives. When they move into relationship with the living God, they will hear God calling them to have some loving impact on the things that are happening in the world.

Learn to read a newspaper with a consciousness of the human dimension of the things that are going on. Has the closing of a plant caused widespread unemployment? Is there a difficult issue before the legislature? Is there crime? Has there been a natural disaster? Is there war? Learn to feel the struggles and the suffering that these things represent. Lift them up in intercessory prayer. Has something good happened? Have you heard of a loving response being made to a human need? Have some oppressed people claimed their freedom? Has something happened that is evidence that God's saving work is being done in the world? Be ready to interpret all of these things in the light of the Christian faith to the people who will gather in your church.

You need to live in constant conversation with the Christian faith and with the witness it makes to the God who meets us in all of the experiences of life. Any person who is committed to living a life shaped by the Christian faith needs to do that. Those who are responsible for preaching and leading worship need to see it as a part of their vocation. The Christian faith provides us with some important witnesses telling us some important things about God and about the loving, saving work God is doing in our lives and in our world. They tell us things we really need to know.

The holy scriptures are primary among these witnesses. The doctrinal heritage of the church is another. The liturgical heritage of the church and the rich accumulation of traditions of worship is another witness that will certainly be of value to those who preach and lead worship. The contemporary witnesses of people in our own day, who have had some experience of an interaction with God and told about it, are really the same kind as the witnesses that have come down to us through the ages. Seek all of these witnesses out. Take them in. Interact with them. Bring them into conversation with your own experiences of life. It is out of that conversation between the Christian witness and life that you will discover what you have to share in sermons and to embody in services of worship.

The study of the holy scriptures should be our primary and constant source of insight into the shape of our interaction with the God who meets us daily in life. The Bible is an awesome collection of the witnesses of people who have experienced interaction with God in different historical situations and in different situations in life. They all come to a climax in the witnesses of those who were close to the event that Christians believe was the definitive revelation of God, the life of Jesus who is the Christ. The church has set this collection of witnesses before us and said, "This is the definitive witness." Yes, it is a collection of ancient books and it will take some disciplined study to understand all that they have to share. But the God to whom the Bible writers witness is still God. The God who was made known to us through Jesus Christ is still a living, active presence among us today. That God is still doing the saving work to which the Bible writers witnessed and is still calling us to the kind of life of loving commitment he called people to in biblical days. Read the witnesses of the Bible writers and you can know what to expect to find God doing in your life and in your world today.

All reading of the Bible can be of value, but there are some ways of reading the Bible that can be of greater value for those who will be facilitating interactions with God. Some people who have a great need to make things manageable have a way of selecting certain concepts from the Bible and putting them together into doctrinal systems. They tend to impose the structure of their systems upon their reading of the Bible. I suppose we all have a tendency to do that, but there are dangers in it. Having decided that our doctrinal system represents what the Bible says, we may never let ourselves hear the Bible say anything else. The Bible is a magnificently vital and dynamic accumulation of witnesses. It is full of complex themes in dynamic tension with one another. Once you get into it, you have a sense that you are dealing with something that is in motion rather than with something that is standing still. It arises out of experiences in real life and out of interactions with the living God. For that reason, it speaks effectively to our experiences of real life in all of their dynamic complexity. It would be tragic for us to put the Bible into some kind of a little doctrinal straitjacket that would keep us from being able to hear its redemptive word. The Bible could speak to some difficult situations in our lives that were not addressed by our doctrinal belief system. It would be tragic if our belief system should become so brittle that it could be discredited or shattered by the impacts of life upon it, when the more dynamic witnesses of the Bible itself could have entered into creative conversation with the things that are going on in our lives.

Let me try to say this in a different way. Our objective should be to lead people into a dynamic relationship with the living God who meets us in life and to help those people discover how that relationship can shape their lives. It should not be just to teach them ideas about God, even ideas with scripture references attached, or to lead them into a life structured by doctrines, disciplines, and rules. Yes, doctrines, disciplines, and rules have their value; they are parts of the heritage that the church has given us for our guidance. But it is best if we relate to them and to the scriptures as guides intended to lead us into relationship with God so that our relationship with the living God can shape our lives.

Do you know the story of Jacob wrestling with the angel (Genesis 32:22-32)? That has been for me a model for my approach to the scriptures and to the other great witnesses of the church. I consider them all messengers from God. I assume that they have something of value to offer to me that has to do with things going on at the deepest level in my life.

I engage them with all of the honesty and attention that I can. I ask them the big questions. I bring my doubts and fears into the conversation, as well as my hopes. And if I am looking toward the preparation of a sermon, I try to bring all of the doubts and fears and hopes of the people who will hear the sermon into the conversation too. I take hold of the messenger, just as Jacob took hold of the angel, and I wrestle with it intellectually and spiritually until it blesses me with some insight, some discovery of a piece of the meaning of what is happening in my life and the lives of others. If I don't discover the blessing in it, I don't just delete it as something that doesn't fit into my belief system. I let it stay there as something with which I haven't yet finished wrestling, something that may yet bless me when I have lived my way into a place where I can receive the blessing.

Like Jacob, I sometimes find myself injured by that wrestling. My precious little belief systems are sometimes put out of joint. But when the wrestling has been fruitful, I come away with a new understanding of who I am and of what life is about. I come away limping but more able to deal with life as it comes to meet me, because I have found my way into a new relationship with the living God. When I am at my best in my sermon preparation, that is the kind of thing that goes on. I believe that when my sermons are at their best, they lead the hearers through a similar kind of wrestling with the messages from God.

Preparation for preaching and for worship should bring the

witness of the Christian faith into conversation with the life experiences of the participants. It will help greatly if those who preach and lead worship learn to live in that kind of conversation day by day. Remember, our objective is to facilitate some interaction with God that will help people discover who it is that meets them in their everyday interactions with life, and who will enable them to live in the kind of relationship with the one who makes their lives all that they can be now and gives them hope for eternity.

Worksheet #1
Beginning the Process

Date of Occasion _____

Type of Occasion _____
(For example: morning worship, Easter Sunday, beginning of a pledge drive, devotional for a prayer retreat, and so on.)

What does the nature of this occasion suggest about the message and the service you will be preparing?

For whom are you planning this sermon and worship experience?

What do you know about the important things that are going on in the lives of these people and this community?

Designing an Order of Worship

The purpose of a worship service is to facilitate a life-shaping interaction with God. Those who have responsibility for leading worship should think things through and plan with the accomplishment of that purpose in mind. A worship service should consist of a series of acts of worship, each of which is intended to dramatize and facilitate some aspect of what the Christian faith has taught us about the ways God relates to us and the ways we should respond to God.

It is not necessary for a congregation to follow an order of worship so rigid that they do the same things every Sunday. It is better if they don't. Variety helps to generate fresh insights. Variety also helps to dramatize the dynamic and multi-faceted nature of our relationship with the living God. But it is good for a church to follow a basic order of worship with which the people can become familiar so they can know what is supposed to be happening and participate with the appropriate commitment and expectancy.

> **Every congregation needs some order
> of worship with which they can
> be familiar, within which
> they can do creative work,
> and from which they can occasionally depart.**

It is good, for instance, for the people to come into the church building thinking: "We are gathering as a fellowship of people who share faith and love." It is good if they can go on to think: "We are becoming aware of God's presence and standing in awe of God's greatness and celebration of God's love for us. We are becoming aware of who we are as we stand in God's presence and trusting in God's love for us. We are being honest with God about our brokenness and our needs. We are listening to hear what God has to say to us. We are committing ourselves to God and to God's purpose for us and for our world. We are going out to serve God in the world." This is the succession of attitudes that gives order to many traditional worship services. If people are familiar with such an order of worship, then they can recognize variations or unique acts of worship as ways of trying to facilitate some special interaction with God that the occasion makes appropriate or in creating a specific differential.

The pastor should take the lead in helping the congregation develop an order of worship appropriate for their unique character and situation. When a pastor comes to a new church, she or he may be tempted just to "correct" all of the things that the church has been doing in its worship services and install an order of worship of his or her choosing. Many pastors, especially young ones, have a hard time understanding why they should not do that. They think: "After all, I am the pastor. I have been to seminary. I have been ordained. I know how worship ought to be done, and I have the authority to do it. Why can't we just do it right to start with?" But in churches, especially small ones, it is much better to exercise leadership than authority. It is better to start with the people where they are, even if some of them seem to be clamoring for change, and then to work with the people over a period of time to develop something better. The worship service that emerges through such a process is likely to be much more creative and appropriate than one that might have been chosen before getting to know the people. The people are then likely to have a much greater sense of ownership and participation in a service they have helped to plan. The word "liturgy" that is often used to denote an order of worship actually means "the work of the people." I will be making several suggestions about how to let it be that.

The basic shape of a service of worship can develop within the worshiping congregation. That is not to say that every pastor and every church should feel free just to "do their own thing" in worship. There is a need and a responsibility to design worship that rightly represents what the Christian faith tells us about God and effectively leads people into the kind of response to God that will lead to fullness of life. There can be a lot of variety in that. Considering the dynamic nature of our interactions with the living God, there actually must be a lot of variety in it. But that shape and that variety must emerge from our ongoing creative conversation with the gospel of Jesus Christ, not just by personal whims or by any notions about what might be popular.

Developing an Appreciation for the Dynamics of Worship

It is important for those who are to be involved in the planning of worship to develop an understanding and appreciation for the dynamics of worship and a feeling for what ought to happen in a service. I will talk about how to help laypeople develop such an understanding. Before doing that, however, perhaps you should ask if you really have a good feel for the dynamics of worship. Lots of us are accustomed to going through the motions that we have been taught are appropriate. It is important for a pastor to have a growing understanding and experience of the deep and complex things that can happen in worship.

> **Remember,
> a worship service
> should be a relational happening
> guided by an understanding
> of the Christian witness.**

We will suggest some studies that can help in developing an understanding of the dynamics of worship. They may be fruitful studies for you. They can be even more fruitful if you lead groups of church members through them.

You might lead your congregation in a study of the worship heritage of your denomination. Go through the rituals and ask why those things are done. Think together about the successive seasons and festivals of the Christian year and how they dramatize the saving work of God in the world. Think about how they can be made to facilitate the worshipers' response to that work and their participation in that work. Suggestions for the worship life of the congregation will emerge from such a study. If you follow a lectionary in your selection of scripture readings, you might invite groups of church members to participate in a weekly study of the scriptures to be read in church. Later, we will suggest that such a study can be a valuable resource in sermon preparation. As you reflect on the discoveries the group makes through such a study, you might ask: "How might we embody that in some act of worship next Sunday?" Let me suggest two additional studies that could be especially helpful in developing an appreciation for the dynamics of worship.

One such study might be a Bible study on the book of Psalms. Besides being a magnificent reservoir of insight into the depths of spiritual aliveness, the book of Psalms was also the hymnal and the book of worship for the Jewish people. The psalms came out of the depths of human experiences, all kinds of human experiences, and out of the depths of interactions with God. They were collected and preserved for the purpose of facilitating the interactions of others with God, both individually and as worshiping congregations.

As you study the various psalms, you might call attention to the different kinds of acts of worship they suggest: processionals (Psalm 100), responsive readings (Psalm 24:7-10), litanies (Psalm 136), and others. Such a study can also call attention to the many different kinds of interactions with God that can take place in worship: songs of trust (Psalm 23), hymns of praise (Psalm 8), laments that are prayers for help (Psalm 22), Torah psalms (Psalm 1), penitential psalms (Psalm 51), prayers of thanksgiving (Psalm 107), covenant renewal psalms (Psalm 81), prayers for the nation's leaders (Psalm 2), and others. Any good commentary can guide you. Reflecting upon these can suggest ways in which all of the various aspects of our interactions with God can be incorporated into worship. Let the study lead you into engagement with the things that are going on in the lives of the participants. That will make the study more valuable to them. It will help them to understand that the things you do in study and in worship are intended to be responsive to their real needs. It can also give you valuable insights that can guide you in your preaching and pastoral care.

Another study that could be helpful might be a study of the one ritual with which most church members are familiar, the service for the Lord's Supper. It provides an excellent example of the fact that worship is designed to facilitate an interaction with the living God. You might start by reflection on the way in which the tangible symbols of bread and wine represent the presence of God and of God's loving outreach to us. At one level they represent daily food, God's wonderful gift of life. When the Old Testament origins are considered, they represent the Passover, God's gift of liberation. Most importantly, they represent God's outreach to us through Jesus Christ. The bread and wine represent everything that Jesus is, was, and did. They represent the broken body and bloodshed of Jesus, God's suffering that proves God's love for us. They represent the new possibility of fullness of life that God makes available to us through Christ. It is important for the people to realize that all of the things represented by the symbols are real and present and available to them. There can be a real interaction with the living God. The worshipers are invited to receive not just the symbol, but the gift of love and life from the living God who is there and ready to give them.

It will be helpful to reflect upon the various aspects of the ways in which we should approach God to receive what is dramatized in the service of the Lord's Supper. There is the drawing near in trust and in love. There is the honesty about our needs and repentance for our sins. There is the recollection of the saving works of God done in the past, especially the saving work done through Jesus Christ. There is the grateful receiving of the gift of God, and there is the commitment of ourselves to God and God's purpose. Reflect on the fact that if we are able to approach the altar in that way, we may actually be able to receive the gifts of love and life from God who waits there to give them to us. And if we learn to approach life in that way day by day, we may be able to receive the gifts of love and life from the God who waits for us there. God waits for us at the altar, ready to interact with us through the experiences of daily life.

As you study the communion ritual, reflect on the implications for other acts of worship as well. What other things might represent the presence of the living God in ways similar to the way the bread and wine do? Could the presence of love in the Christian community do it? How about the reading of the scriptures and the preaching of the word? What else have we learned from the Christian scriptures and tradition about the ways in which we ought to approach God and respond to God? How might those things be embodied in acts of worship? How might the interactions with God happening in worship be helped to shape the interactions with God that happen in our everyday life?

In addition to leading study groups on worship, you can incorporate reflections on the meaning of worship into the expository parts of sermons and into words of explanation and direction in the services of worship. We never substitute a lecture on the meaning of liturgy for a sermon or a learning exercise for a worship service. The sermon and the service have a different purpose from an informative lesson. They are intended to facilitate an interaction with God. But on the way to facilitating that interaction, words can sometimes be spoken that can enhance the understanding, appreciation, and participation of the worshipers.

Beginning to Plan Services of Worship

Most congregations have either chosen or drifted into a basic order of worship that guides their weekly services. This is a choice that ought to be carefully considered and made quite intentionally. It can be a good idea to start by analyzing what the congregation is presently doing in their worship services. Many churches follow an order of worship developed for the camp meetings and revival services that were so important several generations ago. Such services start with songs and prayers chosen to make people feel their need for God's saving grace, then move into a sermon designed to offer that grace and to call for a commitment, and they come to a climax in a call for commitment at the end of the service. Such services have a rich tradition behind them, but do they really meet the needs of a small congregation where nearly everyone has already accepted Christ as their savior? Today, a great number of congregations follow orders of worship heavily influenced by things that are being done in the world of entertainment. Many people are addicted to being entertained. And if the things they do at Branson, Missouri, or in rock concerts can teach us something useful about how to worship, we ought to be ready to learn. However, it is important to remember that our objective is different from that of the entertainment industry. When the service is over, we cannot just ask "Were we entertained?" We have to ask: "Did something important happen between God and us?" A great many churches simply follow the order of worship printed in their hymnals.

Most denominations have basic orders of worship that they recommend. They have good reasons for recommending them. It makes sense to start with that basic order. The United Methodist church, for example, recommends a worship service with four basic parts.

The first part is called the *entrance*. In this part of the service, the people gather as a community of faith, become aware of God's presence, then hear and respond to an invitation to enter into relationship with God.

The second part is called *proclamation and response*. It is made up of hearing the reading of significant selections from the holy scriptures, hearing the sermon, and perhaps receiving other kinds of witnesses to God and to the good news that the Christian faith tells us about God. This segment of the service should also incorporate significant acts of worship designed to dramatize and facilitate the worshipers' response to God.

The third part of the service consists of the *service of the Lord's Supper* or, if that service is not to be included, some other act of thanksgiving.

The last part of the service is the *act of being sent out into the world* to live a daily life that is shaped by a relationship with God and committed to the service of the purpose of God.[1]

This structure for a service is simple and basic. It is patterned after the worship services that were held in the Jewish synagogues where Jesus worshiped. It offers lots of possibilities for designing worship to meet the needs of the people to be served. It is a good place to start.

When worship leaders and worship planners move beyond the choice of a basic order of worship, two tasks should be given careful attention. The first is becoming aware of the possibilities. You need to become aware of the many things that can be done to help worshipers move into life-shaping interactions with God. Many people are only aware of what they have seen done in their own churches since they were children, but there are lots of possibilities. Attention should be given to deciding which of the possibilities could really be most helpful to the people in your congregation and community.

Second, the planning of worship services should be done by a group of church members representing all of the different age groups and other significant groups in the congregation. You might even include some people who are not church members.

> **Let the people
> get in on the action.
> They have a lot to share.**

When you begin to explore the possibilities, it is best to look at the things that the congregation is already doing and ask: "Why do we do that? What need does it meet and what purpose does it serve?" It really is important to develop an appreciation for the things that have become traditional in a congregation and to understand how they are meeting needs. It may also be useful to ask if there are things being done that are really not meeting any needs. But don't be too quick to hand down that verdict. Sometimes the things people do in worship are meeting needs they cannot articulate or of which they are not even aware. If changes are to be made, plans should be made to meet those needs in better ways. The exploration of possibilities should move into a study of the great traditional acts of worship. Probably the best known of these is a unison repetition of the Lord's Prayer. If our purpose is to help people move into a life-shaping interaction with God, we can find no guide better than the outline for an interaction with God that was given to us by Jesus himself.

The psalter is another biblical resource that can be helpful. We have already talked about the ways in which the psalms embody the prayers of people in all sorts of life situations and in all sorts of interactions with God. You might ask if there is a better way of using the psalter than just reading a responsive psalm at the same time every Sunday. What would happen if the psalms, perhaps with a few words of explanation, were moved around in the service and allowed to serve their original purposes, like adoration, confession, petition, or thanksgiving? Explore the great prayers that have become a part of the Christian tradition. For example, the prayer of Saint Francis, "Lord, make me an instrument of your peace," or the serenity prayer of Reinhold Niebuhr, "Lord, grant me the serenity to accept the things I can't change, the courage to change the things I can change, and the wisdom to know the difference." Those prayers have led many people into experiences with God. Explore the great traditional services of worship that have developed in the worship life of the church. We have already suggested studying the dynamics of the service for the Lord's Supper.

Other services can also help us to catch the visions that others have had. There is a great reservoir of traditional acts of worship. They are worthy of your study. Consider also the Apostles' Creed and the other great affirmations of faith. When worshipers stand together and repeat the great affirmations of the Christian faith, they renew their commitment to live the Christian faith and do it in fellowship with believers of every nation, in all ages, past, present, and future. This can be a very significant act of worship.

Exploring the great traditional resources for worship can help those who plan services develop a deeper understanding of the dynamics of worship. It can also put useful tools into the hands of worship planners. However, we should not let our exploration get stuck in the past. Some people seem to think that God only hears prayers that were composed by dead Englishmen. People in our own day are experiencing life-shaping interactions with God as real as those of the saints in ages past. They too are producing resources for worship that can be useful in leading people into similar experiences and embodying right responses to God.

We think of the movement toward what is usually called contemporary worship, which has gained a great deal of popularity. There are many different kinds of contemporary worship. Most of them have the advantage of putting things into language, thought forms, and expressions that seem more natural to twenty-first-century people. Materials from these sources are being published in great quantities. They are readily available. Resources are also available for multimedia worship that can offer some exciting worship experiences for churches equipped to use them. Explore all of these things. Become aware of all of the possibilities.[2]

Don't let yourself be so taken up with the grand and the novel that you fail to see the very simple possibilities that are right before you. "Bill plays a harmonica well. I wonder if he would play an offertory for us now and then." "One of the Sunday school children made a really good drawing of the good Samaritan. I wonder if we could photocopy that onto our bulletin cover on the day when that scripture lesson is read in church." There is no limit to the resources available to help us facilitate interactions with God. Let the exploration of those resources be an ongoing adventure for you and for the people in your church who are involved in the leading of worship. Plan an order of worship that makes room for the use of resources like these.

The next question to be asked is: "Which of the possibilities that are available to us will be most helpful to the people we serve?" As you move into this phase of worship planning, it will be very important to sell everyone involved on the approach to planning that we have called creative faithfulness. You need to help them understand that you really do intend to explore all of the aspects of what the Christian faith tells us about our relationship with God and the worshiping community. Help them understand that you intend to make every effort to do the things that will be most appropriate to facilitate the congregation's interaction with God.

The danger is that some may come to the planning process with their minds already made up that traditional worship or contemporary worship, evangelistic worship or "the way we have always done things" is what is best for the congregation and will always argue for whatever represents that style instead of being open to other possibilities. Not only does that short-circuit the creative process, but it also sets the stage for some conflicts that can be very divisive. You might have your own local version of what has been called "the worship wars," and no congregation needs that. Persuade the participants in your planning process of the importance of real sensitivity to all that is going on in the lives of the people and of real appreciative openness to the possibilities available for use in worship. First, however, persuade yourself.

As you begin planning together, you may need to start by enlarging the scope of your thinking to include not only those who are presently participating in worship but also others in the community whom you hope to attract to your worship services. Some people have a hard time understanding why they should do that.

They say, "This is our church. We are paying the bills. It should meet *our* needs." I have heard older members of a congregation say that about the younger members of the same congregation — never guessing that they were planning the funeral of their church. It may be necessary to spend some time thinking together about the evangelistic mission of the church. That need not lead you too far afield, since the people most likely to be attracted to your church are people who are in some ways like the people who are presently attending your church. Nevertheless, the question needs to be asked: "Are there any things we could do that would make our worship services more attractive and helpful to people who are not now attending our church but who might be attracted to it?" Special attention should be given to making worship services attractive and helpful to young families with children and teens.

It might be good to start your thinking together by making a list of all of the things you know about the people for whom you are planning worship. What is the age range of the people for whom you are planning? What is their educational background? What types of music do they choose to listen to? What do they do during the week? What do they think are the most important things going on in their lives? What are the major sources of stress and distress in their lives? Where do they find their greatest joy? What things in the wider world are impacting their lives either positively or negatively? It can be really helpful to see all of these things written out in a list. Start making the list at one meeting, then let the participants think about it and finish the list at the next meeting. Always be ready to add something to the list. This process should serve two purposes. It should help you get a feeling for the needs that could be met in worship, and it should help you get some ideas about what kinds of acts of worship and what communications of the gospel might be most meaningful and helpful to your people.

Eventually you will have to reckon with the question about what possibilities are really available to your church as a small membership congregation. By all means, start by recognizing the positive aspects of your situation.

> **Start planning your order
> of worship
> by recognizing the positive possibilities
> that are in your situation.**

Small membership churches have a capacity for intimacy and warmth. Pastors can relate to people and people can relate to one another on a close, person-to-person basis. People can call each other by name. There can be a kind of winsome informality about the service, even when a very formal order of worship is being followed. People can share their personal joys and sorrows and ask for the prayers of the congregation in the service. Don't fail to make the most of the positive aspects of life in a small membership congregation. Think about which acts of worship are most appropriate for your church. Be open to all of the possibilities. For instance, a prayer read in unison works just as well for a congregation of six as it does for a congregation of 600. On the other hand, unless you have some really dynamic music leadership, the gospel singing that many people love so well really needs a larger group.

You also have to reckon with the limitations of your situation. Is your building attractive and conducive to worship? Are there some things you could do to make it more so? Do you have the equipment for multimedia worship? Could you occasionally borrow some? It may not take much. Do you have musicians who can lead worship? I visited one very small church with music leadership that really brought the singing to life. I visited another that had to make do with a "boom box" and a recording of accompaniment for the hymns in the hymnal. Such recordings are available from most denominational publishing houses.

Are there any unique possibilities in your situation? I visited one church that worshiped in an A-frame sanctuary. They projected the words of the songs for their contemporary service on the ceiling. It kept everyone looking up. Are there any people in your church who might like to try some chancel drama, any good lay speakers, any people with an inspiring witness to share? Make a list of the resources available to you and keep the list growing.

Take a positive and appreciative attitude toward all suggestions. Very few of the things that people will want to do in worship are actually bad. Most will embody some positive value, some representation of some aspect of the Christian faith, some ability to meet a real need of the worshipers.

The problem with many suggestions is that people want to concentrate on one aspect of the Christian faith rather than developing a balanced diet of worship experiences. The best way to deal with that is not to reject the suggestion. Instead, find ways of incorporating it into the total worship experience in a way that will allow it to make its contribution along with other acts of worship representing the rest of the Christian experience. The biggest exception to that is the unhappy person who insists that the church down the road is really doing worship right and you ought to do it like they do. Keep a positive attitude toward your own denominational heritage and your own congregational identity. Do the very best job that you can of being who you are and offering the unique witness and ministry that is yours to offer.

It might seem that we are just about ready to come up with a formula for putting together a weekly worship service. We can design a structure for a call to worship, an invocation, some hymns, a prayer of confession or some other unison prayer, an affirmation of faith, one or more scripture readings, and a sermon. Then we can go to our resources — the hymnal, the book of worship, and maybe the internet — to choose something we like to fill each space. Plug in the sermon when it is finished, and you have the service planned. It is easy to fall into that pattern of planning a worship service. This is especially true when the choir (if you have one) needs to plan several weeks ahead, the person who types the bulletin needs the information by Wednesday, and the pastor doesn't finish the sermon until Saturday night. I am going to suggest that there is a better way of planning a worship experience.

> **Plan the sermon
> and the worship service
> as one unit.**

Most worshipers experience the worship service and the sermon as a single unit. A pastor and worship committee can do a much better job of planning a unified experience if they plan the sermon and the worship service together. Then it is possible to choose preparatory acts of worship and acts of response that relate to the theme of the scripture lessons and the sermon. It is hard work to do it that way. It requires planning ahead and working with other members of the worship team, but it is a better way to do it. It will produce a more meaningful, unified worship experience.

We are about to leave the subject of planning a worship service and move to the subject of planning the sermons. We will talk about how sermons and worship services can develop together. Later in the book we will come back to the subject of planning and leading an individual worship service. We will also think together about how to plan key parts of a worship service like the pastoral prayer. I will give you a little preview of some of the things we will say about planning the total worship life of the congregation. We will emphasize the importance of painting the whole picture. We must try hard to embody all of the different aspects of what the Christian faith has to say about God and our relationship with God. We will want to relate all of that to the whole range of human needs and experiences present in the congregation that gathers to worship. If you and your congregation are alive and growing in your understanding and experience of the Christian faith, this will make the preparation for preaching and worship an open-ended adventure. You cannot really know where it will lead.

We will also suggest that you not only need to paint the whole picture but to paint it with the whole palette. Consider all of the different possibilities available to you in your situation. Use whatever forms of communication and participation in worship that seem most likely to facilitate your congregation's interactions with the living God on any particular occasion. We will discover that creative faithfulness in planning preaching and worship can result in a rich and varied worship experience that can make a real difference in the lives of the participants.

---

1. *The United Methodist Book of Worship* (The United Methodist Publishing House, 1992), pp. 15-32.

2. Rob Webber and Stacy Hood, *ReConnecting Worship* (Nashville: Abingdon Press, 2004) is a useful resource, though somewhat oriented toward larger churches.

Worksheet #2
Analyzing Your Church's Traditional Order of Worship

Do an appreciative analysis of the order of worship your church follows on most Sundays.

What does your congregation usually do first?

How does this facilitate the worshipers' interaction with God?

What does your congregation usually do next?

How does this facilitate the worshipers' interaction with God?

What does your congregation usually do next?

What does this do to facilitate the worshipers' interaction with God?

Continue asking these questions until you have outlined and evaluated all of the aspects of your church's customary order of worship. Be careful not to be too negative in your evaluation. Many acts of worship serve good purposes that are not immediately apparent.

Are you aware of any strong positive or negative feelings in the congregation about any aspects of their customary order of worship?

Do some "brainstorming." On a separate sheet of paper list as many unique resources and possibilities available to you for varying and enriching your services of worship.

Preparing to Preach

Now it's time to talk about preaching the sermons. That is what most pastors and lay speakers get most excited about. You ought to get excited about it. It is one of your best opportunities to be an agent of the hope of the world. Important life-shaping and history-making things can happen in services of preaching and worship. You ought to get excited about being a part of something like that. You will have to get excited about it so that you are willing to do all of the hard work necessary to maximize the possibilities inherent in the preaching event. Be careful, however, not to fall in love with the image of yourself as a preacher. Lots of us do that. It is a big mistake. This is no place for an ego trip. Rather, this is a place where we can find ourselves by losing ourselves in the service of something bigger than ourselves.

It is important to go back and remember some of the things we said at the beginning about preparing to preach and lead worship. Remember that it is our purpose to facilitate life-shaping interactions with God. It is our hope that something will happen in the service of preaching and worship to change the lives of people and will, through those changed lives, change the world. Remember that people who preach need to live every day of their lives in the conversation between the Christian faith and the lives of the people to whom they will speak. They need to live in sensitivity and in responsiveness to the drama of life going on around them and within them. They also need to live in regular study of the scriptures and of the other witnesses to the saving work of God. They need to always be wrestling angels to see what blessings they may discover that could be shared with those who come to participate in the preaching event, and they need to be constantly open to the presence and the guidance of the living God.

All of that is preparation for creating sermons. The question becomes: "What is a sermon?"

> **A sermon is
> a relational happening
> intended to lead people
> into life-shaping interactions
> with the living God.**

A sermon is an event, a happening. It is not primarily a piece of literature, either written or spoken, even though writing and speaking usually play important roles in it. We have said that we hope to facilitate interactions between the worshipers and God. An interaction is a happening. The worshipers ought to be thought of — and they ought to think of themselves — as participants, not just hearers or receivers. We believe that the living God is present and active. If it is your understanding that it is your job to facilitate an interaction between people and God, then that understanding ought to inspire both great commitment and great humility.

A sermon is a relational event. The best way to facilitate relationships is through relationships. Your relationships with the people are very important. The people need to be able to believe in you. They need to be able to believe that you respect them and care about them and want what is best for them. They need to believe that you are a person of integrity and you believe the things that you are telling them. If people can believe these things about you, they will forgive a lot of inadequacies. This is especially true in small membership churches. You also need to know that in a small membership church, the people will know whether or not you are real. The pastors of megachurches and television evangelists may be able to hide behind carefully cultivated public images. But in a small membership church, the people will eventually know who you are. Be who you are. Be honest about yourself with yourself and with the people and be a person who is intentionally growing in your relationship with the people and with God.

> **Who you are must validate what you say.**

Give some thought to the way in which you will relate yourself to the people and to the way in which you will express that relationship when you are preaching. Will you stand over or against your people and thunder "Thus saith the Lord," or will you stand beside the people and say "Let's try to hear what the Lord is saying to us"? The way you choose to let your relationship with the people be shaped will do a lot to determine what will happen in the sermon, how you will engage the participants, and what is likely to happen in the interaction. Remember, God relates to us in love, and love is the response God wants from us. Love ought to shape the relational setting of every sermon. That is true even of those sermons on the judgment of God. Until you have learned how to preach on the judgment of God in love for the people who are under judgment, you probably ought to avoid the subject. God speaks all of his words, including his word of judgment, in love, and if you can't do that you may misrepresent God.

A Christian sermon should be an event shaped by biblical faith. The Bible is the definitive witness of the Christian community of faith to the reality and the saving work of God. Church members have a right to expect that the biblical witness will shape the messages they hear in church. It will not be enough just to read a few verses of scripture that appear to support what the preacher wants to say. The message should arise out of the whole of the biblical saga and the whole of the biblical message. It will not be possible to get the whole biblical message into one sermon. However, the whole message is implied in every aspect of the message, and every time the preacher speaks on one aspect of the message he or she should do his or her best to be responsible to the whole message. Each message should arise out of serious study, sound biblical scholarship, and reverent obedience. All of the interactions toward which the sermons move people should be aspects of the kinds of interactions that the Bible tells us can and should take place between God and us.

A sermon event should relate the biblical message to the lives of the people who are participating. It is not necessary to know everything that is going on in the lives of all of the people present to relate the message to them in specific ways. In fact, it might be dangerous or embarrassing to try to do that. But if the participants have the feeling that the message is related in one way or another to life in its depth, they will feel it relating to everything that is going on in the depths of their lives. A trivial or superficial sermon, or one lost in theological abstractions, will not do that.

A sermon may take many different forms. Most sermons will take the form of some kind of a monologue in which the preacher stands up and speaks to the congregation. But a sermon can take other forms. It can take the form of a cantata or a sermon in song, a drama, a multimedia presentation, or some combination of those. Anything that occupies the space allocated for the sermon in a service of worship should be a relational event designed to facilitate an interaction between the participants and the living God. It should embody a biblical message and relate to the lives of the participants in a way that can help them move into the kind of relationship with God that the Bible says will lead to fullness of life.

Planning Sermons

I want to talk about planning sermons. That's right, sermons — plural — rather than a single sermon. We will soon get around to talking about how to develop and deliver a single sermon. But for those who are going to serve as pastors or worship leaders of a congregation, it is very important to plan ahead and develop a master plan for preaching. It is good to plan the preaching for a whole season of the church year or even for the whole year. There are two reasons for this.

The first is that pastors need to plan a "balanced diet" for their congregations. A congregation needs for all of the different aspects of the Christian faith to be explored and to be related to the lives of the members. If the pastor just depends on the weekly inspiration that she or he hopes will come, it is not likely to happen. Preaching at its best happens when a pastor is working regularly with a congregation to help its members grow toward fullness of life in faith. Retired pastors often receive invitations to fill in for other pastors who are sick or away. I have frequently heard retired pastors say that there is no comparison between preaching a single sermon as a guest speaker for a congregation of strangers and preaching week after week for several years to a congregation with whom you have a pastoral relationship. That has been my experience too. Planning ahead is part of good pastoral leadership.

The second reason for planning ahead is that it enables you to have several sermons in process at the same time so that you can spend more time working on them. The preacher's worst experience is that of coming to Saturday night and not having a sermon ready for Sunday morning. Maybe the demands of pastoral care or administration crowded out the preparation time. Maybe you are going through a spiritual dry spell. Maybe you have something like writer's block. On Saturday night, you go to your study and sit there looking at a blank sheet of paper waiting for that last-minute inspiration to come, but panic comes instead. Finally, in desperation, you get out a book of sermons written by someone else and pick one to ad-lib as if it is your own. That *will* happen to you if you plan on being able to prepare one or more sermons a week during the week before they are to be preached, and it will not be a good experience for you or for the congregation.

If you set aside some time for long-range planning at the beginning of a year or a quarter or a season of the church year, then you can work on a number of sermons at once. You can set up a notebook with a date, a topic, a scripture lesson, and maybe some other basic sermon ideas written at the top of the page. Better yet, you may set up a box of file folders with that information written on them. You can start by reading the scripture lessons and maybe some commentary on the lesson and spending a little time thinking about the message or messages the text might suggest. Then you can keep the next several sermons you plan to preach in your mind and brood on them. As you have time, you might do more studying or reading on each. Jot down your reflections. Better yet, you can become aware of bits of conversation or stories from the newspaper or reflections that come to you while you are driving the car or mowing the yard relevant to the sermons you are planning to preach. Jot your thoughts down and drop them into a file folder or fasten them to the sheet in your notebook that is for your sermon in process. Then when the time comes to prepare the sermon for the week, you will find you have already made a good start. You will have something to work with. You will be spared the Saturday night panic and your church will be treated to preaching with much more depth and relevance.

The need to plan ahead and provide a balanced diet for your congregation is the best argument for following a lectionary in your preaching. A lectionary is a list of scripture readings recommended for reading in church on each Sunday of the year. In some denominations, a lectionary is prescribed and pastors are expected to read the designated scripture lessons for each Sunday and to preach on them. In other denominations, an increasing number of pastors are choosing to follow the Revised Common Lectionary. The different lectionaries are very similar.

Most of the lectionaries recommend four readings for each Sunday. The first reading is from the Old Testament or from the book of Acts. The second reading is from the New Testament epistles. The gospel reading is from one of the gospels. In Year A, most of the gospel readings come from the gospel of Matthew, in Year B from Mark, and in Year C from Luke. Readings from John are scattered throughout the three years. There is also a Psalm recommended for each Sunday. The lectionary is planned for a three-year cycle. After three years, you start over again.

The scholars who created the lectionary planned so there will be some common theme among the texts recommended for a single Sunday and so that during the three-year cycle most of the important themes and texts in the Bible will be covered. The assumption is that if all four lessons are read in church each Sunday, a person who attends church every Sunday for three years will have heard most of the New Testament read (some passages more than once) and also the most important passages from the Old Testament.

The texts provide readings that are appropriate for the different seasons and occasions of the Christian year, but not for local or national holidays like Independence Day or Thanksgiving. You will have to decide whether you will read all four lessons every Sunday or only the ones on which you will preach. Being a little bit of a teacher, I always thought a few words of introductory interpretation could help a congregation appreciate scripture lessons that are only read.

You will find the lectionary a valuable helper in planning a balanced diet for your congregation. The scholars who planned the lectionary had that in mind. If you tend to be a topical preacher who feels a need to address certain doctrinal teachings or social issues or congregational needs, you may be surprised how well the lectionary anticipates those needs and provides opportunities to do that and scripture lessons on which to base your preaching. I have found when I become deeply concerned about some issue, within a few weeks, the lectionary provides an opportunity to deal with it.

Of course, if there is some issue that needs urgently to be addressed — a tragedy that needs to be coped with, a national emergency that needs to be interpreted in the light of the Christian faith, an issue with which the congregation needs to deal — then depart from the lectionary and deal with that issue immediately. The lectionary should be the servant rather than the master of the worship life of the church.

You will also find the lectionary a great help in setting up your sermon-in-process system. You can start by setting up your sermon-in-process file or notebook by simply writing the lectionary texts at the top of a page with the date on which it will be preached. As you begin to plan for a season of the church year, set aside time to read the lectionary texts. Notice any themes they have in common and any relevance they seem to have to the needs of the congregation. Jot down these initial thoughts on the planning sheet.

As you have the opportunity, begin to read commentaries on the text. You will find that the lectionary frequently suggests a number of successive texts from the same book of the Bible. This can facilitate your study and also suggest the outline for a series of sermons. Many excellent Bible commentaries give specific suggestions for preaching possibilities in the lectionary texts. *The New Interpreter's Bible* and the *Interpretation* series do that. Lectionary study guides are also published regularly by several major publishing companies. As you read these, reflect on them. Ask "What is the message of this text for my congregation?" Write down your reflections. Soon you will find that you have a starting place for a sermon. Work ahead. Try to work on the sermons for a whole season at one time. When the time comes to prepare the sermon for the week, you will find that you have already made a good start. In sermon preparation the old proverb holds true that "a job begun is half done."

> **Plan ahead.**
> **A job begun is half done.**

As you go on to develop your sermons and worship services, you will find that many different resources are being published to assist the preacher. They range from sermon starters, illustrations, and liturgical resources to complete sermons on every text of the year. These can be helpful, especially to a beginner. I hope, however, that you will use them as "pump primers" to stimulate your own creativity, and not just scrap baskets from which you will select pieces to sew together into a quilt. Let the lectionary lead you into creative faithfulness; not into short-circuiting the creative process.

Here is a suggestion: Some of the richest experiences of Christian fellowship and of shared insights that I have ever had came in groups of ministers of different denominations who met together weekly to study the lectionary texts. You might explore that possibility.

Let me share a few reflections on following the lectionary. The lectionary can help you to balance the diet of your congregation and also lead you into exploring new and exciting dimensions of your relationship with God — but only if you let it. If you always choose the most familiar texts and just say about them the things the people have heard many times before, the lectionary will be just a shortcut to getting your job done. But if you let it challenge you to study the less familiar passages and themes, it can lead you into exciting new discoveries that you can share with your people.

I have found it is best to pick one of the scripture lessons to be the primary text for your sermon rather than to preach on all four texts at once. For a while, I tried to preach on all four texts. I spent a lot of time trying to discover the common theme and explaining it to the congregation. I soon found I was producing sermons that were scholarly but not very helpful. Once you have chosen the primary text for your sermon, you may frequently discover that one or more of the other texts will lend itself to playing a supporting role. The balance, tension, and dialogue between the texts can add a real dynamic quality to your message. However, it is better to start by choosing one primary text and letting the focus of that passage be the focus of your sermon and the worship service.

If you choose not to follow the lectionary, then you will need to find some other way of planning a program of preaching and worship that will have the needed balance and allow you to work ahead. A sermon series on one of the books of the Bible can do that. The four gospels and the epistle to the Romans lend themselves to that use. A series on the great themes of the Old Testament can also work well. You may decide to design a topical series on major Christian beliefs or a pastoral series responding to the felt needs of the congregation. Sometimes you may want to publish a list of topics you think might be appropriate and allow the members of the congregation to check the ones they would like to hear. In that way, they can request sermons they feel are needed.

If you take a topical approach to preaching, you must be conscientious about choosing texts that really do speak to the issue you are addressing. Don't just pick a passage that gives you a "pretext" for saying what you want to say. And remember, it is very important to paint the whole picture.

Worksheet #3
The Starting Place

This sheet can be one page in your "sermon in process" notebook. Make one page like this for each sermon you are planning.

Date _____

Occasion _____

Texts:

Read the texts over twice, maybe once aloud, and jot down some key words or a brief summary that will help you remember which text this was. Later, read a commentary on each text and jot down any important insights you gain from that reading.

The Old Testament reading:

The Psalm reading:

The Epistle reading:

The Gospel reading:

Write here your first thoughts about the messages these readings might have for your congregation. After you have spent time in the study of the scriptures, go back and brood over the thoughts you have gathered. Write out summaries of the several messages that these scriptures may have to share. Choose the one that seems most appropriate for your congregation on the occasion for which you are preparing.

Discovering the Message

Now it is time to talk about how to prepare a sermon. The first task that must be accomplished in preparing a sermon is discovering or deciding what you want to say. Fred Craddock, whose book on preaching has been a standard text for many years, spends half of his book talking about having something to say.[1]

We have to keep reminding ourselves that most of the people who come to church are hoping that something will happen between themselves and God. Ultimately, what they want to hear is not the preacher's opinion but rather a word from the Lord.

How do we begin to discover what needs to be said on a particular Sunday? We must start, as we have said, with living in an active and growing relationship with both the living God and the people to whom we will speak. Everything we do must be informed by our ongoing study of the scriptures, the other witnesses to God, and by what we know about the community we serve. In the preparation of a sermon, the ongoing conversation between the biblical witness and the drama of human life and history must come into focus in a unique and personal way.

We have suggested planning a preaching schedule around the texts recommended by the lectionary. If you do, you will have a starting place. There are other places you could start. You could start with some deep human need among your people that calls for a response. You could start with some major moral or social issue that needs to be addressed. There may be some issue in the congregation or the community that needs to be put into perspective, or some need to put a growing edge on some aspect of the faith of the people you serve. Hopefully, you will not use the sermon just to promote a program or to do something else that should have been done in the announcements. Some topics are too weak for a sermon. But if there are some needs that really should be addressed, the first task will be to find a significant passage of scripture that speaks to the issue.

It is important to find a passage that really speaks to the issue and not one that just appears to do so. Also, be sure that the passage rightly respects all of the great themes of the Bible. You can find a few verses that will appear to justify almost anything you want to say. Be sure that you are setting the issue or the need in the context of the total biblical witness. The great danger in topical preaching is that it may be shallow in its grounding in the scriptures. Those passages that are relevant to our contemporary needs are there, but you will need a broad grounding in the knowledge of the scriptures and of biblical scholarship to find them. If you can't find a passage that really speaks to an issue, it may be that you are not yet ready to deal with that issue from the pulpit.

Both approaches to preparing a sermon lead us to begin with one or more passages of scripture. We have already suggested that it is best to start the process of brooding on the scripture lesson several weeks before the sermon is to be preached. Read the scripture lesson. You may want to read it aloud. What are your first impressions about what this passage may be saying to you and your congregation? These first impressions are significant. Write them down, but don't become too committed to them just yet.

It is good to begin reading some commentaries on the text as soon as possible. That will help you to know whether your first impressions of the meaning of the text are leading you astray. It is tough to have some bright sermon idea that you really like shot down by some scholar who shows that you have misunderstood the text. But you need that discipline. Don't say to yourself, "It was such a good idea. No one in the congregation will know." Don't underestimate the intelligence or the biblical understanding of your people. The real issue is the integrity of your preaching. You are called to be faithful to the message of the text.

Then go into a deeper study of the text to discover what the message for the day may be. Read the commentaries. Don't be afraid of critical biblical scholarship. In this case, the word "critical" does not refer to an approach that is negative or fault-finding or intent on tearing something down. Instead it refers to an approach that asks questions about the text and of the text in an effort to discover its message.

> **Don't be afraid to ask questions about the scriptures and of the scriptures.**

Right after finishing seminary, I became the pastor of a rural circuit. There I met an elderly gentleman. He had retired after working for the county for many years, building wooden bridges on dirt roads. On my first encounter with him he said to me, "Preacher, I've read the Bible from cover to cover, lookin' to see who was talkin', who he was talkin' to, and what they was talkin' about. And you know what, Preacher? People ain't livin' like they ought to." I realized that this very down-to-earth fellow had just summarized the meaning of a critical study of the Bible. Asking the questions "Who was talking?" "Who was he talking to?" and "What were they talking about?" can move us far along the road to understanding. Of course, he did not realize how complex things can get when you ask those same questions about the authorship of the New Testament book of Hebrews or about one of the groups of editors who gave us the Pentateuch.

Some people who need the security of keeping everything manageable are afraid to ask too many questions about the Bible. They are afraid they will discover something that will shake their faith. But a faith that has to be protected against honest questioning is already an unstable faith. If we put our faith in the God to whom the scriptures witness, rather than in the inerrancy of the scriptures themselves, then we will be free to explore all of the dimensions of the biblical witness and to discover all it has to show us. In fact, one good approach to preparing a sermon can be to start with the questions your people may have about the meaning or message of the text and then lead them through the questioning to discovery.

When you have done your critical study, don't forget to ask

the bigger question: What is this passage saying to us? When this gentleman reflected on his study and observed that "people ain't livin' like they ought to," he moved from critical scholarship into the field of hermeneutics, the study of meaning and message. This is where we hear God speaking a life-shaping word to us through the scriptures, and that is what the sermon should be about.

The scriptures have many different ways of helping us hear a word from the Lord. Some passages, like the words of Jesus in the Sermon on the Mount, can be taken as words spoken by God to all of us. There are other passages in which the words are spoken by the writers to people whose life situations and experiences are like our own. For instance, if we find ourselves in the same situations in life as the people to whom Amos spoke, or having experiences like those of the Corinthian Christians to whom Paul wrote, then the words of Amos or Paul may very well embody the word of God for us. Some Bible stories tell of the experiences of people who had life-shaping encounters with God. Think about Jacob wrestling with the angel (Genesis 32:24-31), David being confronted by the prophet Nathan (2 Samuel 12:1-15), or the Samaritan woman being confronted by Jesus at the well (John 4). Insofar as we can identify with these people, we can virtually experience their encounters with God as encounters of our own. The preacher who can skillfully lead hearers through that encounter can actually facilitate an encounter with God. Sometimes we can move into similar interactions by trying to understand what the psalmists were experiencing when they wrote their psalms or what Paul was experiencing when he wrote Romans 8.

We can also hear God speaking to us as we reflect on the meaning of the great epic movements and the pivotal events in the biblical drama: the exodus, the exile, the return of the people of Israel, the crucifixion, the resurrection, and the day of Pentecost. What do these stories tell us about God and about what we can expect to find God doing in our lives and in our world today? Spend as much time as you can in deep study of the texts and in reflection on their meaning. You may hear God speaking through the text and through your interaction with the text in different ways.

If you do that, you may very well hear the text speaking several different messages to you and to your people. This is especially true if you have been digging into two or more of the lectionary texts. Then you will have to choose which of the messages will be the message of the sermon. Choose one and save the others for another occasion. It will complicate and weaken your sermon if you try to preach on all of the messages of any text.

Which message should you choose? Choose the one that is most appropriate for your congregation, the one that is most likely to be responsive to their needs, the one that is most likely to lead them into some needed interaction with God. Of course, you will sometimes choose the message about which you can get excited. There is something to be said for that. But when you can, give priority to the message that your congregation needs to hear.

> **Listen until you hear
> the message
> that is right for your people
> on the occasion
> for which you are preparing.**

When you have chosen the message, state it. Write it out in one fairly simple sentence. This is important. It will keep your sermon focused. I was taught very early to start the process of sermon preparation by writing out the topic, the text, the message in a nutshell, and the hoped-for response. I continued to follow that discipline for 45 years. When I have wandered from it, my sermons have suffered.

The summary sentence will state the message that you will want your congregation to hear and take home with them. You will probably include it somewhere in the sermon, perhaps in the introduction, perhaps in the conclusion.

It also helps to write out a statement about what you hope will happen as a result of the sermon. Keep that statement simple too. I suggest one sentence. Of course, you can't completely control what will happen in the sermon. Both God and the people you are preaching to are alive and active. You can't control the interaction between them. But you should have in mind something that you hope will happen. That will help you to decide how to organize your presentation.

The topic is really a summary. It is a few words that help you to know where this sermon fits into the big picture of the Christian faith. Later, you may add a title that will tell prospective worshipers what you are going to talk about in a way that will stimulate interest. Avoid coming up with a cute title and then writing a sermon to go with it.

> **State your message.**
> **Define your purpose.**
> **Stay focused.**

When you have defined the message and the purpose of the sermon, you are ready to start putting the sermon together.

---

1. Fred B. Craddock, *Preaching* (Nashville: Abingdon, 1985).

Worksheet #4
Developing the Message

Title:

Topic:

Text or texts:

Summary of the message:

Expected response (What do you hope will happen?):

List any illustrations or resources you may have available that might be useful in accomplishing your purpose.

Begin to think about the ways in which you might organize a sequence of thoughts or materials or experiences to effectively communicate your message and accomplish your purpose. Jot down several tentative outlines.

Developing a Structure for Your Sermon

When you know what you are going to say and what you hope will happen, the next step is to choose or develop a structure and gather materials that will accomplish your purpose.

Some sermon messages and purposes will best be served by one type of sermon structure and others by different structures. A sermon to motivate may call for a different structure from a sermon intended to edify. I want to start by sharing one model of a sermon structure that you may find useful. A long time ago, a man named Monroe came up with a formula for writing a motivational talk that can be useful in writing many sermons. He outlines five steps in what he called "the motivated sequence."[1]

The first step is the attention step. The speaker must start by getting the attention of the hearers and focusing it on the topic of the talk. This step will correspond to what we will call the introduction of the sermon. This is very important. We will talk more about it later.

Second, the speaker must convince the hearers that there is a need. The speaker may make the hearers aware that they have some need that can be met, or perhaps that there is some need in the world to which they ought to respond. Some use of information and statistics may be helpful here, but it will be more effective to help the people see the human side of the need and identify with it.

The third step offers a solution to the problem or an answer to meet the need. In a sermon, this is where the message of the scripture can be introduced and explained.

The fourth step is visualization. The speaker helps the hearers understand what things can be like if the message is heard and responded to in the right way. A story of something that has happened in the life of a community, some witness telling about the difference that has been made in the life of some person, can help the hearers catch a vision of the possibility that the scripture lesson opens.

Finally the sequence ends with an action step, one that tells the hearers what sort of response is called for and urges them to make that response. Someone said that they like for a sermon to end with the preacher telling the people to go home and bake a cake for a sick friend. Of course, the responses that God calls for are varied and often much more demanding than baking a cake.

Obviously, this sequence will not serve every preaching purpose, but it does give an example of the way in which a sequence of thoughts can be arranged to accomplish a purpose. You may find that it can be adapted to many preaching purposes. It is a formula that can help the beginner get started, and it may be useful in helping even an experienced preacher get going on those days when the artistic muse just won't stir. It can also be helpful to look over any sermon and ask how the functions of attention, need, satisfaction, visualization, and action are being met.

However, if every sermon follows the same outline, the predictability will become monotonous. Fred Craddock, whose book *Preaching* we have mentioned before, suggests that you should become familiar with the many different structures for a talk that have been developed by secular and religious rhetoric so that you can choose one that is appropriate for the message and the purpose of the sermon you are preparing. I won't go into a detailed explanation of all of these rhetorical structures, but the names by which Craddock calls them will give you a clue to what he is talking about. Listen to these names and see if you get the picture.

- What is it? What is it worth? How do I get it?
- Explore, explain, apply
- The problem, the solution
- What it is not — what it is
- Either / or
- Both / and
- Promise, fulfillment

- Ambiguity, clarity
- Major premise, minor premise, conclusion
- Not this, nor this, nor this, nor this, but that
- The flashback (from present to past to present)
- From the lesser to the greater

Craddock says that these traditional forms for a sermon can be useful, but he really prefers a more creative approach to forming a sermon. He suggests living with a text and with a message until they suggest a form of their own that will be appropriate to communicate the message to the particular people who will be gathered on a particular occasion.[2]

> **Choose or create a structure
> for your sermon
> that will effectively communicate
> the message
> and accomplish the purpose
> you have heard and chosen.**

You will eventually need to come up with an outline for your sermon. This may or may not follow the format for an outline that you learned in your English class. That outline may serve you well for some sermons but not for others. What you need is something written that will include statements of the main ideas in your sermon and a design for putting them together in a sequence that will lead your hearers through the experience you hope they will have. You need to work with the message until you have such an outline. Then you can fill in the outline with the materials you hope to use to communicate your message. Throughout my ministry, the format for my preparation started with the statements of topic, text, summary of the message, statement of purpose, and a space left for a title at the top of the page. The outline usually filled the rest of that page and most of another one. I followed the outline in writing my manuscript.

1. Alan H. Monroe, *Principles and Types of Speech* (Chicago: Scott, Foresman and Company, 1949), pp. 307-331.

2. Fred B. Craddock, *Preaching* (Nashville: Abingdon, 1985), pp. 170-193.

Gathering Material for Building the Sermon

What materials can you use to accomplish the task assigned to each segment of your sermon? Whatever you think may work. Clear explanations of big ideas are an important component of every sermon. If you can sum something up in a clear and memorable sentence, you will have done your hearers a big favor. Remember, these statements should be short, potent, and appropriate for oral communication, not the long, complex statements that are appropriate for literature or technical writing. Remember also that your explanations will be more effective if they move down the scale of abstraction toward the less abstract and more concrete rather than moving up the scale toward the more complex. For instance, if you are trying to explain prevenient grace, it is best not to spend much time explaining how that concept relates to all of the other abstract doctrines of Christian theology. It is better to give a concise definition and then explain how to recognize prevenient grace if the hearer encounters it on the way to work the next day.

Information and statistics may be useful, especially if you are trying to sensitize your congregation to some major issue about which they should be concerned. Choose the information and statistics carefully and use them in small doses. Most people have a very limited capacity for absorbing statistics. Select a few facts that will really impress the hearers. If they are likely to be questioned by anyone present, cite the source of your information, then follow with some word pictures or stories that will show the hearers the human reality that the facts represent.

Examples from your own daily experience or that of the hearers will help your congregation to relate. Sometimes you can do this with a little bit of light humor that will help the hearers laugh at themselves. When the subject is the source of some kind of anxiety or suffering or grief, however, the examples will need to be serious. Share your own experiences when they are really relevant, but not too often. Don't let talking about yourself and your family become your standard way of preaching.

Stories are very important components of a sermon. A true story of someone who has experienced either the need that the sermon hopes to address or the possibility that it hopes to offer can go a long way toward carrying the message.

Look everywhere for stories. Look in the newspaper, in the books you are reading, in the things you see happening around you. Look everywhere *except* in the conversations people have shared with you in confidence. No matter how you try to camouflage it, if people hear you telling about things you have heard in confidence, they will be very reluctant to come to you for counseling or friendship when they need it. If there is a story you wish to share, ask permission before telling it and inform the congregation that you have permission to tell it.

A little humor can be useful to establish rapport with the hearers, to give a little relief to a serious sermon, and to put things into perspective by showing what is important and what is not. Just lightening up a bit may be more useful than actually telling a joke — unless the joke really makes a point — and unless you are better at telling jokes than I am. But humor must never be at anyone's expense except your own. Telling a joke on yourself can do good things, but don't ever ridicule or denigrate any other person or group. God loves everyone. To ridicule anyone, even someone with whom you disagree, even an enemy, is a denial of the gospel. Don't joke about things that aren't funny. You can't know who you are likely to hurt.

These are the traditional kinds of materials that preachers use to build sermons. But don't forget to consider the nontraditional materials that are available to you. Is there a person in the congregation who could share a witness that would support the message? Are there two or three or four people who could do a chancel drama to illustrate a point? Could you use a picture on the bulletin cover or a film clip from a recent movie to illustrate a point? If these things are used appropriately and tastefully, they can bring a sermon to life and the hearers will appreciate it.

We have already suggested that you should give yourself enough lead time in preparing your sermon to allow relevant materials to come to you. You will soon learn to recognize materials that might fit into a sermon someday even if they do not fit into any that are now in preparation. Learn to jot those things down and establish some kind of a filing system to keep them until they are needed. Always be on the lookout for materials that could enrich the worship service.

> **Gather materials for a sermon like an artist gathers materials for a collage. Anything that can serve the purpose should be considered.**

There are things you can do, at least occasionally, that can add another dimension to sermon preparation. Consider inviting a group of laypeople to help you prepare the sermon. A group meeting regularly to study the lectionary readings can help you discover what is relevant, what is controversial, and what needs explaining. They can also share some personal insights and experiences that can be incorporated into the sermon. Thoughts shared in a group like this can usually be used freely. When you are preparing a topical sermon on some subject, you may find some people in your congregation who know more about the subject than you do. I once got a request for a sermon on dealing with depression. I was able to recruit two psychotherapists and a person who had suffered from depression to help. I once prepared a sermon series on "Twelve Steps to Wholeness" with the help of several members of the Alcoholics Anonymous group that met at our church. When you invite consultants to be involved, make it clear that they don't have to write the sermon. They will just help you to prepare the sermon. Sermons prepared in this way are often appreciated by the congregation. Don't decide that this won't work in a small church; look to see who you have in your congregation. You may find people with much to share.

When you have gathered your material and organized it around the outline, it is time to write the manuscript. You may think it is not necessary to write your sermon out. I think it is. Writing out your sermon accomplishes several important things. It helps you to word your sentences well so that they communicate what you want to say and do not suggest things you don't intend to say. If a sentence is thought through before it is written down, it is much more likely to say what you want it to say than a sentence that you compose as you are speaking. If you know that you have said something well, you are much less likely to belabor the point and say it over several times. You will speak with much greater efficiency and clarity. You will also find that writing a sermon out will help you plan the length of the sermon to fit the time allocated for it and to allow the time spent on each point to be proportionate to the need. I have found that eight pages of my handwriting or two-and-one-half pages of single-spaced type on my computer will produce about a twenty-minute oral sermon. Planning ahead keeps me from running out of time and realizing that I haven't yet stated the main point of the sermon. If for some reason you need to shorten your sermon while you are on your feet (there are lots of reasons for having to do this), you will find it much easier to do if you can picture the whole manuscript and choose what to leave out.

> **Discipline your presentation.**
> **Make an outline.**
> **Write out a manuscript.**

Three parts of the sermon need to be especially well thought through and worded. The introduction, the conclusion, and the transitions from one point to another. The first thing you say should get the congregation's attention and focus it on the subject. You may use a personal experience, a story, a rhetorical question, or an attention-getting statement. A well-prepared introduction will let the people know that you have something important to say and you are eager to share it with them. The last thing you say should give the people something to remember. It may be a memorable story that illustrates the main point of the sermon, something to think about, a call to action, or a summary of all that you have said. Somewhere in the introduction or the conclusion you should probably include the summary of your message with which you started your preparation. The transition statements that you use to move people from one segment of the sermon to the next will help the hearers to see how the points are related to one another and where you are going. These may be related to the main points of your outline.

When you are writing your sermon out, remember that you are preparing for oral communication, not writing for publication. Imagine yourself saying the things you will say to another person whom you know. If it doesn't sound right in that context, rewrite it. If you intend to take the manuscript into the pulpit with you and either read it or refer to it often, then you might experiment with ways of writing that will help you to follow your script and still look up occasionally to retain eye contact with your hearers. Standard paragraph form doesn't do that very well. Consider spreading the statements out on the page or using different sizes of type or different colors. Remember that you are preparing to speak.

You probably noticed that I said: "If you plan to take the manuscript into the pulpit with you..." You do have an alternative. I have found that by the time I have completed the process of preparation and read the manuscript over several times it comes back to me as I speak without referring to the manuscript. This allows me to maintain eye contact, to move away from the pulpit and walk around if I choose, and to maintain the intimacy of personal relatedness that is so important in small churches. The trick in doing that is not to try to memorize the manuscript. Instead, memorize the outline, the sequence of thoughts and materials that you have thought through, and count on the wording coming back to you when you are ready for it. It usually comes to me, not always and not perfectly, but well enough. The exception is that I never tried to memorize quotations or statistics. I read those from a card. When I inserted additional references to the Bible, I usually read them from the Bible to give them authority. This approach to preaching requires thorough preparation. It also requires concentration during presentation. Distractions or preoccupation can get in the way. This style of presentation enabled me to enter into a more interactive relationship with my hearers. If some nonverbal response from the hearers, or some recollection of something that is going on in the life of someone present, should suggest an in-process modification of what I had planned to say, I am free to do that. This method works for me. You will have to decide what works for you.

In my preaching class, I found that some people were afraid that writing out a manuscript might take away some of the spontaneity of their presentation and keep them from being responsive to the leadership of the Holy Spirit. I think that some people may think it is necessary to turn off your mind and let yourself be possessed by the Spirit. There are certain primitive non-Christian religions, like shamanism that teach this, but I have always experienced the living God interacting with me in ways that required me to do the hard work of thinking, deciding, acting. I can feel God's leadership while I am doing the most scholarly preparation. My suggestion to my class members is an approach to preparation that might give them the best of both worlds. I will share it with you.

Begin by doing the hard work of studying and brooding and praying and reflecting. Then later in the week, find a quiet place and devote two or three hours to finishing your sermon. Take a pencil and a tablet, unless you are more comfortable with a computer than I am, and settle down somewhere where you will not be disturbed. Pray for a clear mind. Close your eyes and imagine your congregation sitting there. Remember all you know about what is going on in their lives and about how they are likely to respond. Then pray: "Lord, let's see how it ought to go."

As thoughts come to you, write them down. Start each new thought on a new line and leave spaces between them. Write in longhand. Don't worry about the spelling. In most cases, no one is going to see it but you. Keep on receiving and writing until you feel like you have it all.

Then it is time to get critical. Don't worry about being critical of God. It is my experience that God speaks to us in terms of insights, understandings, and pictures. We supply the ideas and the words. You are being critical of your own reception, not of God's transmission. Remember, in this context, as well as in the study of the scriptures, being critical means asking questions, not tearing something down. The first question you should ask is the big one. Did this message really come from God or have I been listening to something else that led me off on a tangent? The way to answer that question is to ask yourself if it is in keeping with the Christian witness that you learned from the Bible and the tradition of the church. Could you imagine this message having come from Jesus? If your work passes that test, here are some other questions to ask as you read over your first draft: Are there any statements here that need to be said better, maybe more simply, so that people can understand them better? Are there any ideas that need an explanation, or maybe an illustration, so that people can see how they relate to their lives better? Is this all put together in the best order? Would it flow better if I put this before that or the other over here? Does it build to a climax in the right place? Does it really say what I think God wants me to say, and could it accomplish what God wants it to accomplish?

If there are several revisions, you may want to write the manuscript over, or you may just want to scratch things out and write corrections in those spaces you left between ideas. You can draw arrows to change the order of things. Whether or not you write it over will depend on how big a mess it is. If it is not too bad, you may want to go with it as is. Then look it over, pick out the main ideas, and underline them. That will form your outline. I write my sermons following the outline. You may "find" your outline in the sermon.

When you get through reworking the manuscript, do not try to memorize it. Read it over a few times and count on it coming back to you when you get up to preach. If another thought comes to you while you are preaching, you can add it.

People do things differently, but I have found one thing to be very true.

> **Thorough preparation does not hamper the work of the Holy Spirit. It facilitates it.**

Adding variety to your preaching is something that your people will appreciate and it will keep your preaching interesting. There are lots of things you can do to add variety without completely forsaking the sermonic form. (We have already said it is okay to do that occasionally but not too often.) Experiment with different styles of presentation. If you are preaching on one text or one message that you really want your people to commit to memory, consider using a cumulative summary. In this approach you start by reading one word or one phrase of your text or message and talking about it. Then you read the first and second phrases and talk about them. After that you read the first, second, and third phrases and so on until you finally read the whole text and summarize the message. The repetition helps people remember. You can imagine how you might do this with a text like John 3:16. Using a cumulative summary would get really monotonous if you did it every Sunday, but as an occasional change of pace it can be stimulating.

Consider introducing a second voice into the sermon. If you are working your way through a long passage of scripture in homily style, reading a part of the passage and talking about it and then reading another part and so on through the sermon, consider having a lay reader read the scripture passages. Having both male and female voices in the sermon can be nice. That will give variety. Or you might have another person ask questions that you will answer. This could be exciting if the questions are generated in a meeting of the youth group and asked by some of the young people. Sometimes a sermon can be given in the form of a rehearsed dialogue. This takes lots of extra preparation, but your people will appreciate you for going to the trouble.

Many preachers are rediscovering the art of storytelling as a way of communicating a message. A story is an appropriate way of leading people into an interaction with God. An interaction is a happening. Stories are much better ways of talking about happenings than information or doctrine. In fact, doctrines are more likely to come to life when you tell the stories behind them and the stories of what can follow from them.

Don't be afraid to tell a story for fear that the more sophisticated hearers will be offended. I have had some of my best responses to sermons that started with this introduction: "Today I am going to tell you about one of the revelatory misadventures of Christopher Oddball, who, you will recognize, is an entirely fictitious character made up for the sole purpose of illustrating sermons that might be hopelessly dull without him." What followed was always a satire on the life of some people with whom the hearers could identify. There was humor in the stories but never of the kind that would belittle or ridicule anyone. Everything in every sermon must affirm God's love for everyone. Humor can help us to put things into perspective and laugh at ourselves while still loving ourselves. It can be redemptive. If you do this, keep it light.

Some of the most creative preaching I ever did occurred one year during Vacation Bible School. I was asked to give the opening devotionals when the children were going to be learning about Peter. On a whim, I decided to show up in costume and do a dramatic monologue. I put on a Palestinian costume, threw a badminton net over one shoulder and brought along a whole fish that I had bought at the meat market on the way to church. I started by saying, "Hello. My name is Peter. I am a fisherman. I want to tell you about my friend Jesus." The devotional made such a hit that I knew I had to follow up with something similar on the other four days of Vacation Bible School. What would I do for an encore? That is creativity under duress. Some people do sermons like that occasionally in morning worship.

Your people will appreciate your efforts to keep the sermons varied and interesting.

> **Give 'em a break.
> Do something different now and then.**

Worksheet #5
Completing the Sermon

Title:

Topic:

Text or texts:

Summary of the message:

Expected response:

In the space below, work out a complete outline of your sermon. It can be revised at any time before you deliver it.

When that is done, write out your complete manuscript, giving attention to the effective use of language.

Presenting the Sermon

The time will come for you to stand up and deliver the sermon you have prepared. Do it in a way that is appropriate for the setting.

In small membership churches, intimacy is important. Putting on a grand performance with florid rhetoric and extravagant gestures may seem out of place. Make eye contact with as many people as you can and try to relate to them. Talk to them as if you were talking one on one. In that setting, you may emphasize a statement by saying it more softly or more slowly rather than by saying it more loudly. Some preachers are very proud of developing their own unique pulpit style. Forget about that and concentrate on communicating the message most effectively to the people with whom you are working.

> **Think of the people as participants
> in the preaching event.
> Help them to think
> of themselves in that way.
> Develop an interactive style
> of preaching and leading worship.**

Let's talk about stage fright. This is a problem that plagues beginners and slips up again on seasoned preachers when they find themselves confronted by new, difficult, or very important occasions. A certain amount of stage fright is normal. It simply honors the importance of the occasion. There are some techniques you can use to deal with it. Pick out some friendly looking people scattered around the congregation and speak to them. Their affirmations will encourage you. If you begin to panic, slow down, breathe more deeply, and give the panic time to pass. A little humor can relieve the tension of a situation. The most important thing to do is to try to lose yourself in the task of communicating the message. Much of stage fright comes from anxiety about self: "How am I doing?" "What will the people think of me?" "Will I make a good impression?" The best thing you can do is to forget about that. Concentrate on the message and the task of communicating it to the people gathered in front of you. Trust God for the affirmation you need and lose yourself in the important thing that is happening. This usually works.

A sermon is intended to lead people into an interaction with the living God that can change their lives and turn them into change agents in the world. That is always a live possibility because the living God is always present, active, and working toward that end. Don't ever forget that. Stay excited about the possibility that is present in every situation of preaching and worship. Study diligently and be faithful to the message that comes to us through the biblical witness and the witness of the church. Be as creative as you can in relating the message to the people who will come to hear. Give it your best. Leave the results to God and to the people you have led into God's presence. You may never know the results of your preaching, but you can know that the one who fed thousands with the lunch that a little boy shared can do great things with the best efforts of a preacher who is committed to him.

Telling stories during the sermon can be an important part of preaching, whether the story is meant to illuminate the text, to illustrate a part of the sermon, or to serve as a whole sermon in itself. People relate to stories because they are all living stories of their own, and they hope to find in other stories some insights into the meaning of their lives.

> **Tell stories that can help people discover the meaning of their own stories.**

Here are some thoughts on how to tell a good story. If the story is to be a biblical story or a story *based* on a biblical story, start by studying the scriptures well. Know the background, geographical, cultural, and theological content of the story itself. Some things need to be told accurately.

You may also use a story that comes from history, from published fiction, from someone's personal experience, or from your own imagination. If the story is one you have made up, let the hearers know that.

Live with the story until you understand how it represents some aspect of the drama of divine-human encounter. Then discover where that story intersects the drama in the lives of the hearers. It is essential to know that. It is your reason for telling the story. The divine drama will interpret the meaning of the human drama and call for some response.

There are many ways of letting a sermon or a part of a sermon take the form of a story. If the scripture lesson tells a story, you can simply tell it again in a way that will help your hearers recognize its relevance. How might you tell the story of Jonah in a way that would enable your hearers to identify with the reluctant prophet and hear God's words to Jonah as words addressed to them? There are stories behind the stories in the Bible. Why do you suppose the author of the book of Jonah told that story? How might you tell his story in a way that would speak to your congregation? Do you know a story about someone who heard the message of the book of Jonah and took it seriously? If you don't, can you imagine a story of someone who might have done so?

Decide how you are going to tell the story. Who is going to be talking and how much information will the person talking give to the hearers and how much will be left for the hearers to figure out for themselves? Writers call these concerns "voice" and "point of view." For instance, will you speak in the third person, viewing the story from the outside?

A lonely woman trudged down the road to the well outside of Sychar Samaria. It was midday and she was hot. Her shoulders slumped. She looked dejected. Suddenly she looked up and saw someone sitting by the well.

Or will one of the characters, the "protagonist," be speaking in the first person?

Great goodness, it's hot. I really hate coming to this well in the middle of the day. It was so nice when I was a young girl living with my parents and when I was a newlywed. Then I could come in the morning with the other women. They were always glad to see me then. We could sit and catch up on the gossip before going back up the road. I couldn't do that now. Those self-righteous biddies would make me miserable. Hey, who is that sitting there by the well?

If you tell the story in the first person, you can let the hearers in on the personal thoughts of one person. If you tell it in the third person, you can tell the hearers what each of the characters is thinking or you can let them look at the story from the outside and guess what is going on. You have to make some decisions about that, and you need to be consistent through the whole story. You also have to be consistent in telling the story either in the past tense or present tense.

Your story needs to start in some way that will get the hearers' attention, generate interest, and suggest that something is coming that will be worth hearing.

Joseph wondered if he would ever see his father again.

Jarred stood watching the cloud of black smoke rising from a place only a few miles away. He knew that he was witnessing a major industrial accident, but he had a gut feeling that he was seeing something of even greater significance.

There needs to be a plot that will lead the hearers through the building of tension or conflict to some resolution; or through mystery to some discovery. Tell the story with enough detail to help the hearer know how things would look, smell, and feel if they were there on the scene. Try to help the people see pictures and experience happenings rather than just hearing words. Use short sentences, active verbs, potent nouns, and few adverbs. Make it move.

Soon after the story reaches its climax, unless the meaning has become clear, you need to be ready to help the hearers discover what the story has said about the divine-human encounter and to explore the implications for the hearer's life or community. If the meaning is very clear, you can just leave it for the hearers to digest without talking it to death.

Stories and other illustrations should help the hearers to understand what the speaker is talking about in very concrete terms. They should help the hearers visualize in terms of pictures and happenings and experiences they can recognize from real life. They may help the hearers identify with the needs being addressed or to be sensitive to the needs of others. They may evoke some virtue or love in the hearer that needs to be surfaced, liberated, and affirmed. They can also help the hearers visualize what things would be like if the called-for response is or is not made. All of these stories and other illustrations should help the hearers to visualize the divine-human encounter and experience their participation in it.

The story should not just illustrate the message, it should embody the message. The message should probably be stated somewhere in the sermon but don't attach it like the moral in one of Aesop's fables. It's important to learn to tell a good story.

How to Preach on Controversial Issues and Survive

If you are conscientious about preaching the whole Christian faith, you will eventually come to some of those messages in the writings of the prophets, in the teachings of Jesus, and in other parts of the scripture that have uncomfortable things to say about the ways in which people are living — including your people — and call for changes that people are not anxious to make. God calls you to communicate those messages to the people because God can use your preaching on these issues to change lives and to change the world. This is often not a popular thing to do. It can get you into trouble. For the first quarter of my ministry, I stayed in hot water most of the time because I felt compelled to say something about the race issue that most of my people didn't want to hear. There are other big issues that need to be addressed like materialism, economic justice, war, and peace. God is not through changing the world, and those who are called to proclaim the gospel are still called to be some of his agents in doing that. But how can we preach those important but unpopular messages and still survive? Let me give you some suggestions.

First, work from within a pastoral relationship in which the people know that you love them and care about them. Months and years of faithful pastoral care when your people need a loving pastor can buy you some credit that you can spend on talking about things the people don't especially want to hear.

Pick your battles carefully. You can only get away with stirring things up three or four or maybe five times a year. Plan ahead to deal with the most important issues. You may need to plan an agenda for dealing with big issues that will be several years long. Then be sensitive to the congregation's felt needs. There will be times when the people will want you to help them understand some thorny issue in the light of the Christian faith.

When you are dealing with a really controversial issue, base what you have to say on the great biblical themes like love and justice. A flimsy proof text will not do. Let the people know they are dealing with something that is the essence of their faith.

Speak from a posture of "withness," not "againstness." Stand beside the people and say: "Let's hear what God is trying to say to us." Don't stand over against them and say: "This is what God told me to tell you."

If you can, involve other members of the congregation in the conversation that produces the sermon so that the message emerges from the congregation's dialogue with God. If the issue is ambiguous, recognize that. Help the people to see both sides of the issue and to think it through in the light of Christian faith. Acknowledge and respect those who disagree with you on the issue. Stay in dialogue. Don't just shut the opposition out as if they were the enemy. They too are people who need to be won. Listen to them, just in case they are at least partially right.

Use humor carefully to lighten things up. If people can laugh at themselves without feeling that they have been ridiculed and if you can laugh at yourself this can put things into perspective, but don't ever ridicule any person or position.

If there are political issues with which you feel you must deal, focus your preaching on principles and issues, not on people or groups. Only in the most extreme cases should you endorse or criticize a person or a proposal as a part of your ministry. Practice your own citizenship conscientiously but privately.

Be sensitive to the feedback you get after dealing with a controversial issue. You need to know where your congregation stands. You need to know when they are ready to move ahead. Your objective should be to move your people to take some action in the service of truth, justice, and love.

> **Preach on controversial issues
> from a posture of "withness"
> rather than "againstness."
> Stand beside those to whom you are speaking.**

Preparing a Service of Worship

It's time to go back and finish preparing the worship service. You and your worship team may be developing the sermon and the service at the same time. It will soon become apparent that you need to be planning ahead in your preparation of worship services, just as you do in your preparation of sermons, so that you will have time for creative ideas to bloom and to be developed. There needs to be an ongoing conversation between the two processes so that when both are finished, you will have a sermon and a worship service that work together to move the worshipers through the experiences you hope to facilitate.

As you begin to complete your preparation for a particular worship service, you should have a basic structure for a service that has become familiar to your congregation. You should also have a basic message and a purpose you hope to accomplish that has emerged from your early stages of sermon preparation. You must now ask how you can most effectively lead your particular congregation through the experiences you hope to share with them. Are there any reasons to depart in any way from the customary order of worship? Are there things going on in the congregation, the community, or the world that might suggest a secondary theme for this service of worship? Is there a last-minute change in the purpose for the service? How will you plan a series of acts of worship that will engage the people where they are and move them into the interaction with God that you hope will happen? You should come up with a series of experiences that you hope the people will have. Then you will select or create or facilitate the songs, prayers, witnesses to the word, and other acts of worship that will help the people have those experiences.

Let me share with you the process I went through to prepare

one particular series of services. In seminary I had been told that a service of worship should follow the sequence of experiences that Isaiah reported in Isaiah 6:1-9. It should start with adoration, an experience of standing in the awesome and loving presence of God: "I saw the Lord sitting on a throne, high and lofty...." This should move us to an experience of our own brokenness and unworthiness. A prayer of confession should follow: "Woe is me! I am lost, for I am a man of unclean lips and I live among a people of unclean lips." Then there should be an experience of God's forgiving love: "Now that this has touched your lips, your guilt has departed and your sin is blotted out." Then there should be an experience of hearing a word from the Lord that calls us to a new life: "Whom shall I send?" The service should end with an act of commitment: "Here am I; send me!" For years, many of my classmates and I organized all of our worship services around that sequence of experiences. It is, in fact, a good example of what it means to plan a service made up of a series of acts of worship intended to facilitate a certain interaction with God.

Later in my ministry, I became dissatisfied with that structure for a worship service. It does indeed facilitate one particular interaction with God, the one represented by the concept of atonement. It addresses our guilt and puts us in touch with God's response to our guilt. That is the forgiving love of God. But I began to realize that guilt is only one aspect of the human need that cripples our lives, and atonement represents only one of the aspects of God's saving response to our needs.

I began to be fascinated with the many names by which Jesus was called. I came to believe they represented stories that the biblical witnesses told to describe their experiences with God. They began with a great variety of human needs and they described a great variety of saving works of God as God responded to them in ways that were appropriate to their unique needs.

For example, those who called Jesus the "Word" were probably people who had been groping to find the meaning of life and experienced Jesus as one through whom God told them what they needed to know. Those who called Jesus "Messiah" or "Christ" were probably people who felt boxed in by hopelessness and experienced Jesus as the bringer of a new possibility. Those who called him the "Son of Man" or the "Prophet" were probably people who needed to be shaken out of an old way of life and moved to repentance and openness to a new possibility. They felt that Jesus had done that for them. Those who called Jesus the "Servant of God" may have been people lacking a significant purpose to live for. They saw Jesus living a life of complete commitment to the purpose of God and calling them to follow him and do likewise. There are other such biblical witnesses to the saving work of God.[1]

These examples will give you an idea of what I was seeing. I decided to prepare a series of sermons on these biblical witnesses to try and help people discover how God's saving response might relate to their own unique needs. Some variations of the attention, need, satisfaction, visualization, and action sequence lent themselves to the development of the sermons. I tried to vary the structures enough to avoid monotony. The services also needed to be designed to move the people through the experiences that the various biblical witnesses described.

Each of these services began as the church was accustomed to beginning, with a time of gathering designed to help people feel welcomed into a loving fellowship. Members of the youth fellowship greeted those who came and gave them bulletins. Adult greeters helped visitors find seats. Announcements were made and people were invited to greet one another. Then a brief prelude played by a musician gave the people a chance to settle down and think about being in the presence of God.

I designed a special responsive act of worship to begin each of these services that combined the call to worship, an invocation and confession of need, and a promise of salvation. Here is an example of one that might have been used to introduce the service where we focused on the saving work of Christ the servant:

Pastor: Jesus said to those whom he wanted to be his disciples, "Come and follow me."
People: What does that have to do with us?
Pastor: The invitation is addressed to you.
People: But we are awfully busy people.
Pastor: Are you busy about the right things? Do you have a

purpose in your life that is big enough to be worth living for?
People: We are not sure.
Pastor: Let us pray.
All: Lord, we confess that we are moving through our lives, sometimes driven, sometimes drifting, but not always knowing where we are going. Come into our lives and give us a purpose worth living for.
Pastor: Jesus said, "If any want to become my followers, let them deny themselves and take up their cross and follow me. For those who want to save their life will lose it, and those who lose their life for my sake will save it" (Matthew 16:24-25).

After such a call to worship, everyone knew where the service was going. Then there was a song. The first song was always familiar, either upbeat or strong, and if possible one that praised God for the saving work to be the focus of the service. We found that the book of Psalms offered responsive readings appropriate for each theme, either a lament that embodied a prayer for salvation or some other form of psalm that spoke of the saving work of God we were thinking about. Other acts of worship were chosen that either witnessed to the saving work of God or embodied the appropriate response a person might make. I ended each service with a "sending forth" statement challenging the people to live their lives in response to the saving work we had been talking about. For example, "Go out now and live your daily lives in the service of the purpose of God, and know that God goes with you to enable you and to lead you into fullness of life." Afterward the congregation sang a benediction with which they were familiar.

I had one regret about this series of services. I was leading a Bible study on the saving works of God at the same time, but I failed to arrange it so that I could have the group members help me prepare the services. They might have helped by composing the opening responsive act of worship. They might also have helped me to visualize the needs we were addressing, and they might even have been able to contribute some personal witnesses to their experiences of God's saving work.

This is one example of an experience in planning a series of worship services. It was just a modification of the order of worship I learned in seminary. Don't let yourself be confined within this structure. Ask what succession of worship experiences would most effectively accomplish the purpose of your service. How, for instance, might you plan a service for Thanksgiving or for Easter that is intended primarily to be a celebration? How might you design a service for the Sunday after some tragedy has happened in the community in which the purpose is primarily to comfort and encourage? Services with different purposes will call for different orders of worship and different acts of witness and participation.

Be careful not to let anything become traditional that should remain flexible. Some preachers distribute an outline of their sermons with blanks to be filled in as the people listen. That is a very good idea when you are preaching a sermon that is intended to teach a certain body of information. Others follow their sermons with a time for questions and discussion. That is a very good idea when you are trying to stretch people's understanding on some big issue. (Believe it or not, it is a very good idea when you think some of the people may disagree with what you are saying.) Many churches follow a ritual borrowed from the revival days that ends with an altar call and an invitation to make a personal commitment to Jesus Christ. That is a good idea when there are people who need to make that kind of commitment. But what if you are leading a service that is intended to lead people into some pensive or celebratory experience? In those cases, the three traditions I mentioned could get in the way. Try to maintain enough flexibility so that you can choose the acts of worship appropriate for the occasion and leave the others for other times.

Again, involve members of the church as often as you can. I offered the members of my preaching class some extra credit if they would recruit some members of their churches to help them think about how they could translate the message and the purpose of the sermons they were preparing into services of worship. Those who did it were surprised and delighted with the results. One group suggested that the pastor try to state the message of Easter in a way that a child could understand, then they helped him think it through. Another suggested a very meaningful way to end a service. Still another developed a creative visual center for the service of worship, then decided that they should do it regularly. All were happy to help in choosing the hymns.

If you are lucky enough to have children and young people in your church, you should do whatever you can to make them feel like a part of the church and to provide worship experiences that will meet their needs.

Even if there are only a few children, they can be incorporated into the worship service. Let them light the candles or serve in other ways as acolytes. Let them sing as a children's choir and don't be too concerned about the quality of the performance. It is the involvement that counts. The idea of having a children's time or children's sermon is controversial. I think it is a good idea. No, it is not enough for their Christian education, but it makes them feel like they belong. That is worth whatever little interruption of the dignity of the service it may cost. I actually count on the children's time to lighten things up and give some needed comic relief.

Look for ways to involve the youth too. One of the best ways to do this is to invite the youth fellowship to plan and lead a worship service once or twice a year. If you do that, don't just pass out parts for the kids to read. Invest the energy necessary to evoke and use their real creativity. Plan to meet with the youth fellowship for at least six weeks before the service is scheduled. Spend a couple of weeks helping them to understand the meaning and dynamics of Christian worship. Then spend a couple of weeks exploring the meaning of the theme of the service they will prepare. Lead them in studying the biblical resources and in discussing their relevance. Invite them to get creative about putting the service together. Once you have convinced them that you actually will let them do almost anything that will serve the purpose of the service, they can get really creative. I will never forget the Christmas service in which the youth group contemporized and dramatized the story of the birth of Christ as if it had happened in the county charity hospital. (The wise men who came were Spiro Agnew, who was then vice president of the United States; Werner von Braun, the rocket scientist; and Ross Perot, who was at that time a rising young prodigy in the computer industry.) On another occasion, they prepared a multimedia presentation to use as a prelude for a

Pentecost service. That enterprise will provide the young people with a great learning experience, hopefully under the leadership of their pastor, and it will provide the congregation with an innovative worship service. Most people will be glad to receive anything that the young people offer.

Once the service of worship is planned, it will be important to get everyone "on board" to make it happen. If you have not planned the service with the help of a worship team, you will need to be sure that everyone who is to participate in leadership knows what you hope to accomplish and what is expected of them. Someone will need to type a bulletin or prepare resources to be projected on a screen to enable the congregation to know what is happening and to provide them with any materials they will be expected to read.

At some time during the preparation, you should give thought to the kind of "ambiance" the service will require. Will it be bright and cheerful, pensive, or perhaps serious? Will it move through a series of moods? Ask yourself what this suggests about the way you and other leaders will behave. What should you wear? How should you move around? What sorts of expressions should be reflected in your face and voice? These subtle things make a difference.

You can see that preparing a worship service with the help of a team and planning innovative acts of worship is a lot more work than the way services are most often prepared. It requires you to look ahead. It requires you to think creatively. It requires you to spend time getting together with others. However, it provides a much more vital worship experience, and lay involvement adds an exciting dimension. Realistically, you are probably not going to do it this way all of the time, especially in a small membership church, but do it as often as you can. And have these processes in the back of your mind when you are doing a solo job of preparation. You will eventually learn to do most of them spontaneously — but don't do it too spontaneously. Don't let yourself drop into a rut. Keep thinking things through, and as often as you can, try to do something special.

Let me give you two admonitions concerning the preparation of services of worship.

> **Paint the whole picture.**

The worship life of the congregation should apply the whole Christian witness in all of its many varied aspects to the whole life of the people and the community who are being served by the church. This will take a huge amount of study leading to an understanding of all of the personal and social, devotional and intellectual, moral and evangelistic, demanding and enabling aspects of the divine-human interaction. The Christian faith is very complex, and your people need to hear about all of it and have it all embodied in their worship services. It also takes a huge amount of sensitivity to all of the things that are going on in the lives of your people and of the community and the world in which they live. Your people need to have the callings and the resources of the Christian faith applied to all of their needs. You will have to be intentional in planning each service and the whole schedule of services to do this. It will be hard work, but it is important for you to paint the whole picture.

> **Paint with the whole palette.**

We have talked about all sorts of things that can be done in a worship service. There are the great traditional acts of worship and also the many forms of Christian celebration and witness that have emerged in recent years. There are also possibilities that have not emerged yet because they are waiting for you to think of them and use them. Go to the other side of the world, if you can, to see if there is something that could be enlisted to facilitate the worship of your church. But don't overlook the simple little things right there in your hand. Consider all of those things to be available to you for the facilitating of the worship life of your church. Don't get locked into always following one style of worship. Creative faithfulness invites you to use whatever God provides to you that seems useful and appropriate for facilitating a life-shaping interaction between people and the living God. Paint with the whole palette and you will come up with something really beautiful.

---

1. James L. Killen Jr., *Who Do You Say That I Am? Reflections on Jesus, A Personal Reader* (Macon, Georgia: Smyth and Helwys, 2002).

Worksheet #6
Complete the Worship Service

Remind yourself again:

What message do you hope this service will communicate?

What kind of interaction with God do you hope to facilitate?

What kind of experiences might you provide that would help people to enter into the hoped-for interaction? How might you organize them into a meaningful succession of experiences?

Can your traditional order of worship be adapted to lead people through this succession of experiences? How?

If not, how might you organize a special order of worship that will accomplish the purpose? Outline the order of worship that you intend to follow.

What special resources are available that you can mobilize to accomplish the purpose of the service?

Make a list of the things that will have to be done to make this service happen, and identify the people who will be asked to do them and who will do the asking.

Preparing Prayers

The pastoral prayer is an important part of a service of worship. That is the part in which the pastor or leader takes the worshipers directly into a personal interaction with God. We should give some attention to that act of worship.

It is important to start with a definition. A significant thing happened one day while I was orienting a new intern, a seminary student who was to work under my supervision for a year. I had taken him into the sanctuary to talk him through the things he would do as a liturgist, assisting in the leadership of worship. When I came to the pastoral prayer, I said something like "Remember that when you are leading the pastoral prayer you are talking to God on behalf of the people in the congregation." I didn't think much about that superficial explanation. I went on and talked about the other parts of the service. When I finished, the intern said, "You know, you have really helped me today. You have explained that when you pray, you are talking to God. I had never understood that before." I was amazed. He was a person who was older than most seminary students. He was two thirds of the way through a seminary education. He had plenty of experience and intelligence, but he had come from a tradition where most prayers were read. It had just never registered to him that when you pray, you are talking with God. Let's start with that understanding. Let's also start with an understanding that God hears our prayers. We can't always expect God will do everything we ask God to do, but we can believe significant interactions take place between ourselves and the living God when we pray.

The second part of my explanation to the intern was also important. When you are leading prayer in a service of worship, you should try to incorporate the feelings and needs of the people in the congregation so they can pray with you. A pastoral prayer is a prayer made on behalf of a congregation, but such prayers are at their best when the people can feel that they are praying along with you.

> **A prayer that will be used in worship as a prayer of the people should be prepared with the same kind of thoughtfulness that goes into preparing the sermon.**

It has often been said that the Lord's Prayer is a model prayer, a prayer given to teach us how to pray. The elements of a complete prayer are incorporated into it. Let's review those elements. There is an address that sets the stage by recognizing and owning our relationship with God, *Our Father in heaven*. There should be some adoration of God to remind us that the God we are talking to really is God, *hallowed be your name*. There should be both submission and commitment to the purpose of God for yourself and for the whole creation, *your kingdom come, your will be done, on earth as in heaven*. There can be petitions. We are invited to ask God for the things we really need, *give us this day our daily bread*. There should be repentance and prayer for pardon, *forgive us our sins as we forgive those who sin against us*. There should be prayers for God's saving grace and for guidance in our daily lives, *save us from the time of trial and deliver us from evil*. The Lord's Prayer ends with an ascription that is an act of praise and a renewal of commitment, *for the kingdom and the power and the glory are yours, now and forever*. These are the elements of an interaction with God that should appear somewhere in a service of worship.

You can have the people pray this prayer in unison; that is a good thing to do, but there are lots of other ways of embodying these kinds of interaction.

You may lead a prayer that you have thought through and written out. Your prayer should gather up all of the deepest concerns of the people in each of the categories included in the Lord's Prayer and lift them up to God. You can also incorporate prayers related to the theme of the service. Don't try to hide little sermonettes to the people in your prayers. Have you heard someone leading prayers say "Lord, we know that..." and then go on for several minutes telling the people something he wants to tell them? Count on God to know all of these things. Concentrate on lifting the concerns of the people up to God. Then allow some time in silent receptiveness so that the people can receive the Lord's response.

Other forms of prayer can be included in a service of worship. Invocations, prayers of confession, collects, and other kinds of prayers can be printed in the bulletin or projected onto a screen for the people to read. If you include a prayer of confession, remember to include promises of pardon too. There can be prayers in which the pastor lifts up a series of petitions and the people make some unison response. Some of the psalms lend themselves to being used as unison prayers. Some prayers can be sung and that can be a beautiful thing.

There are several ways in which a leader can facilitate the participation of the congregation in prayers. Some of them work especially well in small membership churches. The pastor can ask the people to lift up their joys and concerns. He can jot them down and include them in the prayer. Or the people may lift up concerns by saying aloud: "Let us pray for..." and then explain the concern in one sentence. The people can respond in unison, "This is our prayer." When inviting people to list their concerns, it is good to include the great concerns about events that are going on in the wider world that should be of concern to Christians. Don't let it be only a list of everyone's relatives who are in the hospital.

Sometimes, instead of a spoken pastoral prayer the pastor may lead the congregation through a period of guided silent prayer. Ask the people to be quiet within and to visualize themselves in the presence of God. Then suggest the things they should lift up to God in the intimacy of their personal relationship. After each suggestion, allow time for the people to pray. Try to include a variety of prayer experiences in the prayer life of the congregation. Different people will find different kinds of prayer meaningful.

We have been invited to open ourselves to God and to be honest with God about all the things that are going on in our lives. If preaching and worship are intended to facilitate life-shaping interactions with God, then the times of prayer in worship should be the times when those interactions become most intimate.

Worksheet #7
Preparing a Pastoral Prayer

After each of the following headings, write the sentences you will incorporate into the pastoral prayer. Use language the people might be able to think of as their own.

How will you address God?

How will you enable the people to present themselves to God?

How will you state the prayers you know that your people are most eager to lift to God?

How will you lift to God prayers about things that are going on in the world that ought to be of concern to caring people?

How will you represent the people in acts of thanksgiving?

How will you invite people to open themselves to things that God might want to say to them?

How will you lead the people into other aspects of an interaction with God that are important?

How will you enable people to make commitment of themselves to God?

In what order will you offer these prayers?

How will you end the prayer?

Preaching and Worship in the Real World

You have read my book on preaching and worship in small membership churches and you are enthusiastic about putting your new skills to work. You get yourself and your best effort at a sermon all prepared, and you go eagerly to your first service in the first church of which you are to be pastor. Then suddenly you are confronted with an unexpected reality. Things are not like you had thought they would be.

You come early to greet the people. You ignore the fact that the building is in bad repair, has a musty smell to it, and you wait for the people to come. After all, they are what is important. They begin to arrive individually and by families. They are mostly older people. They are eager to talk to the new pastor, but several of them seem a little apologetic. They are discouraged. They can remember when their church had an average attendance of 200 but now it is down to about 40. They explain that many people have moved away, and some of the younger families are leaving to go to larger churches with better programs for their children. One lady confides, rather loudly, that she really liked the last pastor and she can't imagine that you will ever be able to fill his shoes. This is the lady who, at the end of your next service in the church, will hand you a sheet of paper noting all of the grammatical errors you have made in your sermon.

Your spouse has come with you and has taken a seat on one of the pews, but eventually a person comes in and asks your spouse to move so that she can have the seat where she always sits. You notice that all of the people talk to you but that some of them don't talk to one another. The former pastor had warned you that two families in the church are having a feud that has gone on for years. No one can remember how it started, but now they disagree about everything. One family sits on one side of the church and the other on the opposite side. They try to get everyone else to line up with them. When the former pastor told you that, you didn't believe it. Now you do. You notice a young couple coming into the church with three young children. It seems that everyone is looking at them as if to ask "What are you doing here?" You go to greet them and learn that they are first-time visitors. You try to make them welcome and find them a seat. You ask if the seat is usually occupied by anyone else, just to avoid embarrassment. It is a few minutes after church time and the pianist arrives, all out of breath and obviously flustered, and begins to play the prelude without speaking to anyone. You start the service. In the middle of the first hymn, the patriarch of one of the leading families arrives, marches down the center aisle, and asks your spouse to move again. During the invocation, one of the young children in the newcomer family fidgets a little and an older lady sitting behind them says to her husband, in a whisper that can be heard all over the church, "I wish that woman would make her children behave." By this time, the joyful enthusiasm that had filled you just an hour ago has melted away. You are pushing yourself to finish the sermon. And you are wondering what in the world you have gotten yourself into.

Wait. Don't quit yet. This is not really a description of any one church. It is a composite of all of the horror stories I have ever heard from pastors of small churches over the years. Hopefully your first church won't be anything like that. But to be realistic, all of the exciting things we have been talking about have to be done, if they are done at all, in the real world, where not all of the church members embody the combination of spiritual saintliness and artistic creativity for which you have been hoping. What should you do when you find yourself up against some discouraging reality?

It is important for you to keep on believing in the possibility that is present in every situation of preaching and worship. Keep reminding yourself that the living God is present and ready to be responsive, and the people, although their motives may not be entirely pure, have in fact come to church, at least half hoping that something good will happen there between themselves and God. Keep reminding yourself that under those circumstances significant things *can* happen. Remembering that and constantly recommitting yourself to that possibility needs to become a spiritual discipline for you. Some of the people will have come desperately wanting or needing some excitement and some vitality in their worship service. Sometimes you have to be the one who will initiate it.

Another thing you can do is to get to know the people in your church and community. The worship service is one expression of the total life of the church. In a small membership church, the relationship between the pastor and the people is an important aspect of that life. And in a small membership church it is entirely possible for the pastor to build a personal relationship with all of the members of the church and many of the other people in the community.

When you get to know the people, you will come to understand the hurts and the fears behind some of the negative aspects of their personalities. The annoying things that people sometimes do may be expressions of their need for the saving grace of God. These things are part of your assignment as pastor. Knowing this can completely change the way you will relate yourself to them.

As you get to know the people, you will get some insights into the kinds of preaching and worship experiences that may be appropriate for your people. It has been my experience that you don't have to wonder about that. They will tell you. It may be that they do not yet know what creative possibilities you have to share, but at least you will know where you have to start with this particular group of people. We have talked a lot about creative faithfulness. It is through getting acquainted with your people that you can get your creative faithfulness oriented.

It is in getting acquainted with the people that you discover the talents, insights, creativity, and leadership ability people have to contribute to the process of preparing for preaching and worship. In some situations there will be a little bit, in others there will be much. In all situations, there will be some. Whatever you find that is what you have to work with as you develop liturgy that really is the work of the people. Don't stop looking. Many people have lamps hidden under baskets. The more you look for talent, the more you will find. And the more you enlist people's talents in the service of worship, the more worship is likely to become important and meaningful to them.

Most important, as you get to know your people, look for spiritual aliveness in them. Recognize that spiritual hunger is a kind of spiritual aliveness. When you find aliveness — and you will — you may find someone with a witness to share or leadership to offer. When you find someone who is spiritually alive you will certainly find someone with whom you can share the ministry of God. You will need that. It will make you know that you are not alone. That is important. When you find a spark, blow on it.

When you get to know your people, you can talk personally with them about any problems that need to be resolved. Don't thunder from the pulpit about those inhospitable people who won't let visitors sit in their favorite pew. Talk to them personally about the importance of making visitors feel welcome. If there are conflicts and divisions among the members of your church, work personally toward reconciliation. It is not easy work, but there is much more at stake than just an appearance of harmony on Sunday morning.

When you find yourself involved in conflict or when you find yourself receiving criticism, stick to the high ground. Don't get caught up in petty things. Remember that it's probably not about you. Try to overcome evil with good. Work things out through personal relations. If necessary, come to terms with the fact that some people are not going to like you. Since you know that God loves you, you should be able to handle that. Minister to those who don't like you just as to those who are your best friends. Above all, keep your personal conflicts out of the pulpit.

In a small membership church, much of your leadership in preaching and worship and in every other aspect of the church's work, will be done through personal relationships. In personal conversations, share your insights and your visions, your hopes and your misgivings. Try to explain them, and see if people are buying into them. Listen to their reactions. Listen to see if they have some creative ideas and if they are ready to take some initiatives. Work with the people to build consensus and enthusiasm. That is how leadership happens in small membership churches. That is how you get things done.

Through this process you should be learning to love your

people, and as you do, you will enable them to love each other. People want their churches to be loving fellowships. If you can bring some love to the situation, you will be helping that to happen.

By now I hope we have come to recognize what really is important in the worship life of a church. It is not the specific things that are done in a service of worship, it is the intangibles. When people look for a church, most do not set out to find a church that has "high church," "contemporary," or "evangelistic" styles of worship. Instead they look for a church that seems to be alive, one in which they might indeed expect something significant to happen between themselves and God. They look for a church in which there is a warm, loving fellowship into which they might be welcomed. If they have children or teenagers, they look for a church that will have an attractive program for their children. A church that wants to attract new people must be intentional about organizing not only their worship services but every other aspect of their church life to meet those needs. There should be an openness to any innovation that will help the church do that. Just doing something different in a worship service will not, by itself, make the needed difference.

We have talked about the skills needed to give leadership through preaching and worship. We said that many people come to church seeking some intangible things: a loving fellowship, vital worship, the possibility of having something important happen between themselves and God. You will need to give constant attention to your own spiritual formation, because you can do a lot to bring those intangibles to the people who will gather under your leadership to worship God. Remember that God is there, and the people have come hoping that something will happen between themselves and God. In situations like that, exciting things can happen.

> **Stay excited about the possibility that is always present when people gather to worship the living God.**

www.ingramcontent.com/pod-product-compliance
Lightning Source LLC
LaVergne TN
LVHW051657080426
835511LV00017B/2614